5/7/09

Dr. Jason

Make it Happen,

Don Dulles

Also by Dallas Humble

True Prosperity: Acheiving Success in a World of Failure

MAKE IT HAPPEN

STRATEGIES FOR ACHIEVING PEAK PERFORMANCE IN YOUR LIFE

DALLAS HUMBLE

NANCE PUBLISHING
SWARTZ, LOUISIANA

Published by The Nance Publishing Company
Swartz, Louisiana
USA

For inquiries to the author or other information, correspond to Dallas Humble at 3602 Cypress Street, West Monroe, LA 71291. Call (800) 282-1947 ext. 150 to order additional copies of this book.

For information on the Nance Publishing Company write to P.O. Box 188 Swartz, LA or call (318)343-1130. On the Internet email info@nancepub.com or visit our web site www.nancepub.com.

FIRST EDITION

Back Cover Photo by Patty Stewart

Library of Congress Card Number: 00-108835

ISBN 1-888189-04-5

Printed in USA

To my mother.

Thank you for teaching me how to make things happen in my life by instilling in me the qualities and the desire to be a peak performer. I love you.

Contents

A NOTE FROM THE AUTHOR

Dear Reader,

There is nothing more gratifying to an author than to know that what he has written has touched the life of the reader. It is my sincere desire that what I have expressed stimulates you to become all you were created to by achieving peak performance in your life. The purpose of this book is not to change you but rather provide a guide whereby you may find the tools and the willingness to make progressive change in you life.

I would appreciate any comments or suggestions you may have about the book. I would love to hear from you. Have any of these principles assisted you in becoming a peak performer? Do you know of others that I may share in my seminars or future writings? I would love to hear from you.

I hope you will take advantage of the opportunity to expose this book to your friends and associates in the near future. You could make the difference between them winning and loosing in business and at the game of life.

Your comments are appreciated and I do hope to hear from you soon. May God bless you.

Make it happen!

Dr. Dallas Humble

INTRODUCTION

Life is full of desires. It is also full of people attempting to accomplish feats that they never seem to complete. The purpose of this book is to give you a full understanding of what it takes to make things happen in your life and be a peak performer. To perform at your peak requires skills that few are aware of.

At one time in my life I didn't think I was capable of doing what others did. I wasn't a football hero in school nor was I a class favorite. What I was in my mind stemmed from my lack of understanding that I could do anything, within reason, that I put my mind to. At the age of 13, I enrolled in a school of martial arts and began studying karate. I remember our instructor telling us we could do what we wanted to, be what we wanted to be and go where we wanted to go. That is, if we wanted it bad enough. Those words never left my mind. They inspired me. From that day on, I vowed not to quit.

I received my first-degree black belt at the age of 16, unusually young for that time. From the pinnacle of that accomplishment, I became motivated. I knew I wanted to make something of myself. When the time came, I moved a thousand miles away to attend college. After receiving my doctorate, I set up practice in my hometown. At on point I had over 20 clinics. Now I travel speaking to doctors sharing my success and how I learned from my mistakes.

Years later I looked at those hard decisions as some of the best I made in my life. They were all difficult steps, but they all paid off. They all had their costs, but their rewards made it worth it. Looking back on my life, I realize that I could not have done any of this without the strategies I am going to share with you throughout this book. I say all of this simply to let you know that if I can do it *you certainly can.*

In 1959 God breathed into my mother's womb and created me for a reason. He did the same with you. Most of us allow life to pass us by. We believe tomorrow will always come. We can dream, desire and want, but without *doing* the end result will be nothing. There is simply no reason for anyone not to breathe the breath of life and taste a little of what success can offer. First, however, we need to possess three things: the willingness to learn, the ability to change and the permission to fail. With those under your belt you are on your way to making things happen in your life.

There are several things to realize before proceeding. First, you really were born to win. Second, no one is better than you, and conversely, you are no better than any one else. Finally, *you* are responsible for your success or failure, no one else.

As I travel around speaking at conventions and seminars, it astounds me seeing the number of frustrated people unable to make things happen in their lives. They all say they want their life to be different, yet many are unwilling to sacrifice anything to get it. They would prefer to *let it happen* rather than *make it happen.* We will discuss this thoroughly later on in the book.

There are several certainties in life. One is life will go on whether you want it to or not. The other is that we can merely "exist" allowing life to create our destiny here on earth, or *we can create a life for ourselves.* It really is that simple.

What do you want to be known for? If you could be remembered for one thing what would it be? After you have answered that, I'll ask the hard one. Are you living today with the vitality and richness that is depositing in others what will become their good memories tomorrow? If not, why?

Sometimes the truth is tough to face. With courage, facing up to where we are today reveals how to change tomorrow.

To *Make It Happen,* as the title implies, centers on the ability to realize your dreams and goals, to accomplish whatever you set out to do in a timely, efficient and organized manner. Whether you want a better business or personal life, striving to do your best at all you involve yourself in will bring you gratification. It is said that those that die with the most *toys* win. It is my prayer that after you read this book you will realize that those with the most *joys* in life are actually the winners.

This is a book of strategies. Each strategy is a core principle that has allowed me to make things happen in my life. Looking at the table of contents, you will find that each strategy has a specific place in the overall picture of achieving peak performance. To C-H-A-N-G-E Y-O-U-R-S-E-L-F is, for all practical purposes, the secret to any meaningful success.

Most resist change to the point of completely avoiding it altogether. I challenge you to find one individual that has achieved meaningful success or made a significant impact on the world that avoids change. That doesn't mean they may not be set in their ways. What I am saying is that they are open to changing when it is necessary to accomplish their goal.

When I first contemplated writing this book, I wrestled with the name for some time. Finally I realized that to get anything done in life you generally have to make it happen. These strategies are set forth for you to follow in an easy to read manner that, if implemented, will make a positive change in your life.

After consulting with doctors and individuals from around the country, I have come to the understanding that we all have a common denominator when dealing with getting things to happen in our lives. That common denominator placed in a jar and shaken up will come pouring out as these fourteen simple strategies for life. I intentionally made sure the first letter of each strategy spelled the words *change yourself.* I want to drive home the point that without change, the missing ingredient in many lives, you only have a book, nothing more, nothing less.

I have laid out for you fourteen strategies that will, if followed, make you a peak performer in all aspects of your life. Amazingly, many people blame their lack of success on other people. Believing they are doing what it takes to produce results, they assume it must be someone else's fault.

As I have said before *you* are responsible for your own actions. There is no one to blame and nothing to point a finger at. Too often we get caught up in a cycle of "blame games" that only results in disappointment and frustration. Understanding that only we can take advantage of opportunities may prevent this. Yes, there are certain uncontrollable factors, but we are the ultimate "end of the rope."

It is my prayer for you that after reading this book you feel a sense of confidence that you have never felt before. You can be a peak performer and achieve results in your life that you never dreamed possible. The "secrets" are unfolded for you in the upcoming pages. Strategy by strategy reveals the keys to unlock the talent you have hidden within yourself. You will learn the importance of changing, having a vision, possessing passion and determination. You will read about being focused, exemplifying leadership, and bringing out your real potential. I'll discuss how to overcome obstacles and experience a fulfilling life, goal attainment strategies, and wealth accumulation strategies. Latter strategies will show you how to overcome fear and to effectively communicate and what "lifting" is and how you can avoid "leaning."

CHANGE YOURSELF

15

STRATEGY 1 : COMMIT TO : ADAPTING : & THRIVING

Sometime ago a Charlie Brown comic strip had some simple yet powerful words concerning how we view change. Lucy said she would like to change the world. Charlie Brown asked how, and she replied she would begin with changing him!

People for the most part do not like change. They come into a situation wanting to change everything but themselves. The problem is always "out there." It is never "in here." Throughout this strategy we will investigate the whys as well as the hows of making change a reality. There are two main things that we change in our lives. The first is how we feel about something. The second is our behavior, such as our eating habits. The best kind of change will ultimately be progressive in nature.

Not all change is progress, but all progress is change. Even though most people resist change, it is life to the peak performer. We all must confront change at one time or another. To reach any level of achievement in this life, change is inevitable.

Do you want to see progress in your life? Do you have goals in your life, dreams you want to come true? I believe you do. Change challenges people to grow and be different. Change is something the majority of people resist and fear. It is, however, a blessing. It is life. If we seek out positive change, we come to know ourselves better. We grow. We become more confident improving ourselves and enhancing the world around us. By changing we turn today's pain into tomorrow's gain. We become progress makers. Progress makers simply make progress their only viable choice. If we choose any other option, we are choosing to be progress takers, settling for living off other's progress.

Progress makers realize that tomorrow will never be different unless they change. They do not make a change without a plan. The plan may change with the circumstances, but they continue to follow it.

To be a peak performer your interest should lie in creating a life, not just living one. How can you keep pace with all the change and remain sane? The answer lies in understanding the difference between living and just existing. To live means to create. To merely exist means to stagnate. If you're living, you are continuously planning without becoming complacent. True living does, however, breed contentment. To be satisfied with who you are is good. To become lazy is not. If you are going to perform at your peak, change will be part of who you are rather than who you want to become. In order to realize the significance of this statement a few things need to be considered.

- Where do you want to be in 1, 5, 10 years, and beyond? (The Plan)
- What will it take for you to get there? What sacrifices will it take? (The Cost)
- Are you willing to make those sacrifices for a better tomorrow? (The Payment)

Some plan but don't figure the cost. Others take a wild stab at the cost but don't plan. Most choke on the payment. The just can't sign that check.

"I'd like to go back to school, but it takes too long."

"I need to make a certain amount of money, but I am not comfortable doing what it takes."

Time goes right by these people. When it does they'll be that much older with nothing to show for it. Just talking about somewhere will never get you there. If you continue doing the same thing, assuredly you will continue to see the same results.

Two plus two equals four and will continue to equal four until the end of time—unless we change the equation. Many people today use what I call "death equations."

"If only tomorrow..."

"Someday I will..."

"One day let's..."

"One of these days I am going to..."

"When I get this weight off I will...!"

To perform at your peak it is important that you act on the things that change your life. The purpose of this book is to make you act, to do what it takes to succeed. You have made the first move to a better life by reading this book.

Most people desire someone to hold them accountable and guide them on the path to success. There is only one catch. You and you alone must make it happen. Changing ones thinking begins the routine of real change.

- When you change your thinking, you change your beliefs.
- When you change your beliefs, you change your expectations.
- When you change your expectations, you change your attitude.
- When you change your attitude, you change your behavior.
- When you change your behavior, you change your performance and ultimately you change your life.

The mistake many people make is waiting for their circumstances to change their behavior, instead of changing with the circumstances. Quit thinking times are bad. Begin looking at your life as a new and exciting challenge. Be a peak performer by embracing the concept of becoming a progress maker. Environments change, industries change and regardless of what others may say, people do change.

Managed care caused significant changes within healthcare profession during the 1990s. Doctors have literally lost their practices because they were unwilling to adapt to manage care. They wanted to continue running their offices as they did in the 80s. The times wouldn't allow it.

The "mom and pop" stores are another example of resisting change. They are now replaced with bright lights, gasoline, and food. Their variety appeals to the public at large. Those that were motivated to change with the times survived. Those that weren't are extinct.

Motivation means movement. It means tapping into the unlimited power given to you by God and moving forward. It means making a difference, advancing ourselves and those we contact.

If we are motivated, we become passionate about what we are doing. Standing still is not an option. We then focus our attention on improvement while energizing ourselves. We create a momentum that builds the confidence and self-esteem necessary to make change a reality.

If we remain the same, we start feeling complacent. Soon if we are not careful the greatest obstacle success and change have ever known will raise its ugly head. That obstacle is known as fear.

When fear places its death grip around you, doubt soon becomes the rule rather than the exception. We doubt abilities and become overwhelmed with the changes around us. We begin fighting for the illusion of security, failing to recognize that true security lies within us.

Change doesn't require a miracle. It just requires a little faith and a willingness to learn. Do you want to grow? Are you willing to try something new?

As I write this book, I realize that if I am going to produce the work I desire, I must change. I talk about change in my seminars all the time. As a matter of fact I open them up by saying the prerequisite to attaining success is the willingness to learn and change. Without those foundational understandings, information from the seminar is a waste of time.

Do you believe we are destined to change? Do you resist change? These are questions I commonly ask people attending our seminars. Inevitably 80–90 percent say they resist change. Consider this yourself. Is change something you resist? We now realize that people are destined to change. We are engineered to grow and succeed, physically, spiritually, emotionally, and mentally. Should we loose sight of this fact, we convince ourselves that change is bad. We unknowingly place limits on our lives. If you are to succeed, you have to embrace change with optimism and enthusiasm. Those who fight what is natural ultimately lose the battle.

Stop and think for a moment. Are you tapping into your full potential? Are you organizing your time efficiently? Time management is one area that most people could use a crash course in.

Throughout my career I have encountered more individuals with a lack of desire to make changes in this area than almost any other.

Think about how you spend your time. Is it as productive as it could be? Do you FIND yourself getting caught up in unimportant matters, working hard and getting nowhere? Most people never realize that their real enemy in life is their inability to sort through the clutter and realize their full potential.

Are you result oriented or task oriented?

That question answered honestly can tell whether you are a busy person or one that is more interested in "working on" the project before them. I have pondered many hours about why one employee can finish their work almost effortlessly while another is always busy but never completes a task.

The seemingly busy one is always asking for help. They constantly seek more help if you continue to give it. I call it the "busy syndrome."

I have come to understand something about the "busy individual." If they do not allow for change in their lives there is little hope for them in the workplace or in their ability to become a peak performer.

The Power of Perception

In order for us to really make change a reality in our life we must examine how we perceive what lies before us. It is not the change that people actually resist. It is the perception of the change. Two things essentially motivate people: pain and pleasure. If a person is convinced that there is pain in staying the same or pleasure in changing, creating a desire to change their life takes little effort. A simple illustration of this could be exercise. One could view exercise as positive while another views it as a "next to death" experience. These perceptions give people a reason to pursue a particular activity, or to resist it. Therefore if you are trying to change, it is the perception you must sell to yourself.

Peak performers tune into their ideas, visions, and the actions they want to implement. By learning to develop positive perceptions you will learn to accept change.

Have you ever stopped to ask yourself why you are doing something? Many people continue to do things simply because they always done it that way. Rather than considering why they are doing something, time is often wasted doing unnecessary activities. To continue the ongoing change process, people need to ask *why*. Asking why forces us into deeper thinking. It challenges people to question assumptions that eat up our time. We then discover opportunity for improvement.

Being a peak performer carries with it risk. Peak performers turn risk into results. They are not afraid to take chances. Peak performers possess imagination and spirit. They do not lack courage, conviction, responsibility, or character. They walk in integrity and with a perception that stimulates change. They advocate excellence and thrive in adversarial environments.

Without change we limit ourselves in all areas of our lives. Are we standing still or moving forward? To be effective we give to others. We add value and, fill needs. We solve problems and help people. We cherish the fact that we have the ability to change and make a difference in life.

Here is what I want you to do. Think of what you have desired to do for years. Places you would like to go and changes in your life you would like to make. Think of where you desire to be in five or ten years from today. Now write these things down and place them in a conspicuous place where you can refer to them. Afterwards use the following three rules of accomplishment to create an action plan to experience some forward movement in you life.

The Positive Rules of Accomplishment
1. Read the list three times a day (change it as often as necessary)
2. Think of what you want as often as possible
3. Do not talk to anyone about your goals or plans

Now start acting on it! Remember, a bend in the road is not the end of the road, unless you fail to make the turn. Begin now doing the things you have been procrastinating for years. Be a progress maker and create the life you desire. Proverbs 13:4 says, "The sluggard craves and gets nothing, but the desires of the diligent are fully satisfied."

Peak performers are diligent, realizing that the right kind of pain produces pleasure, the kind of pleasure that lasts for a lifetime. Change only takes place when we link it to a given situation in our nervous system. Below are the five master steps to change. By following these simple steps you can make change a reality in your life. Before proceeding to change a given situation, ask yourself, Will these changes enhance my life and make it better? What do I really want?

I believe these questions must be answered honestly to make change last. For instance if the changes I think I want to make do not enhance my life they probably will not last. By the same token if I "think" I want something but really want something else, change won't be permanent either. You may buy a quarter inch drill bit, but do you really want the drill bit or the quarter inch hole it will produce?

Five Master Steps to Change

Decide what you want and what is preventing you from having it. You can't be vague. We talked about what you wanted earlier, but did you really dig down deep inside yourself. If you're sure you know what it is, what is preventing you from having it? Be clear on exactly what is stopping you, for example fearing the pain it will take to change than the pain you'll experience from remaining the same.

Next, face your fear. Fear is the greatest obstacle to your success. Facing it is also the greatest character builder you will ever encounter. You will find that when you face your fears they will become smaller until they cease to exist. Fear is the sheep in wolves clothing. Once confronted it changes from something that could eat you to something you can eat. Learn to confront your fear. Peak performers eat fear for breakfast.

Last, make a decision to do what it takes to follow your plan of change to the end. Making a decision, even if occasionally wrong, is better than never making one at all.

Make change an absolute must.
You can change if you really want to, but thinking about what you should have done won't accomplish anything. Don't *should* all over yourself. Realize a lack of change almost always results in mixed association with your nervous system. You need to gain leverage on yourself. You can do so by first making change exciting and then associating pain with not changing. If someone placed a gun to your head and told you to do something you would never do otherwise, you would probably do it. That's leverage at its max. Change is 80 percent why and 20 percent how. Make your why non-negotiable.

Do something unexpected or different.
Have you ever been talking to someone and been interrupted forgetting what you were talking about? That's interrupting a pattern. If you are to render a pattern useless you must interrupt it in some way by doing something unexpected or different. If it's an argument perhaps it's whispering a private message in the other parties ear. I once heard of someone that told her spouse to make pig sounds when he ate! That may be a little extreme, but you understand the power the unexpected has on our patterns and habits.

Condition yourself until the change remains constant.
Patterns are frustrating to break. After you make a change there will be subconscious pressure to revert back to the old way. I recently built a new office. Often I've caught myself driving to the old one. I had to condition myself, reminding myself over and over again, to drive to the new one. Rehearse the change repeatedly until you conquer your giant, whatever it may be. Then and only then will you be ready for the last step.

Test your change.
The last step in making real change in your life is to test what you have done. Check to see if you ever revert to an old habit. Stay alert to unconsciously switching back to an old pattern. If you can, test yourself and keep score.

cHANGE YOURSELF

25

STRATEGY : HAVE
2 : A
: VISION

I once heard a story about a little boy that wanted to learn what life had to offer. A wise old man took the little boy out in a boat to teach him the priorities of life. After paddling a short while the old man leaned over the boat and scooped some water in his hand. He asked the little boy what he knew about water to which he replied, nothing. The old man told the little boy he had missed out on one-third of life.

Later the old man saw a plant in the water. He asked the little boy what he knew about plants to which the little boy again replied nothing. The old man informed the little boy that he had missed out on another third of life. A short while later, the old man reached into the water and grabbed a rock. "What do you know about rocks my boy," the old man asked. The boy frustrated with this type of questioning answered abruptly, "Nothing, sir. I know nothing about rocks."

Shortly thereafter a loud noise came from the distance. The little boy suddenly jumped out of the boat. The old man stunned by his action, yelled at the little boy, "What are you doing?" The little boy answered, "That's a waterfall you are hearing, and you are about to miss out on the rest of your life!"

Often we fail to realize our dreams because we don't see what is up ahead. Like the old man in the story, we can't see the danger before us. We all need a dream. We need something to motivate us to go on. We need something to shoot for, to aim at, to steer by. The old poet John Masefield wrote, "All I ask is a tall ship and a star to steer her by."

What we dream for is our vision. It is what we aim at. But seeing that dream as obtainable, catching that vision as ours, is visualization. It is seeing how to get to our goal, how to realize our dream. It is our "star" to steer by.

Visualization is seeing what we desire so strongly we can smell it. It is as if we already have it in our own hands. Getting there is no problem. We see it and know how to get there. Visualizing our dreams allows us to plan. It allows us to set the priorities required to make the plan work.

There is a picture of a little boy titled, "Priorities." Perhaps you have seen it. The caption reads, "A hundred years from now it will not matter what my account was, the sort of house I lived in, or the kind of car I drove. But the world may be different because I was important in the life of a child."

Often we fail to realize our dream because we have our priorities mixed up. We focus on things that take us further away from our goals rather than closer. Your focus may be on something distracting you from your goal. Developing visualization requires proper ordering of your priorities.

In order to be a peak performer you must be able to see past tomorrow. Robert Schuller, pastor of the Crystal Cathedral has a life story dealing with creating something out of nothing. After seminary he left for California to establish a church. He dreamed of a very large church made of all glass. Just he and his wife—and of course God—against the world. Of all places he ended up at a drive-in theater!

All the many years he spent overseeing that church he never gave up on his dream. His priorities never changed. He got closer to fulfilling his dream of the Crystal Cathedral by building a large following. When he eventually received his first bid he felt as if his world had ended. It was millions more than he expected it to be. This is a prime example of what happens to many of us pursuing our dreams. Seemingly insurmountable obstacles arise.
We have a choice at that point. We either quit or continue toward our goal. No matter how impossible the dream, we go forward.

Dr. Schuller continued to press onward. He laid out a plan listing all his options. One stood out. Call on people to donate money for each windowpane in the new church. His plan succeeded raising enough money for the construction.

He never had any more problems, right? Wrong! Just when we think we have the tiger by the tail, life's mountains rise up and block our view. When all of his plans seemed to fade away, his chief executive officer told him something that he said forever changed his life. It's wise advice for all of us. He shared that he must do three things: 1. Decide what you must have. 2. Decide what you should have. 3. Decide what you want.

Many get these mixed up. We choose what we want, not what is required to make things work. Often what we want leaves us unfulfilled.

Dr. Schuller continued to see his dream come true. He breathed it. He saw it in the morning waking up. He saw it all day long. Today the Crystal Cathedral is one of the most beautifully constructed monuments. It shows what God-given vision can do. Inside of us lies a pearl that God has placed deep within. A dream is ready to come out. The question is when will we realize it? When will we be ready to walk in it while He develops and nurtures it?

God won't do it until we take responsibility for the valuable jewel He has lent us. He once told a man to "write the vision large and clear." Write it legibly, so that others can read it and catch the vision too (Habakkuk 2:2). God never gives us something without the responsibility to go along with it. He expects us to do something with it

A path has been paved for us to follow. There is a story of a little boy that needed a bucket of acorns for a school project. The night before it was due his dad, frustrated with the boy's last minute request, sent him out with a bucket and a lantern. His dad told him that the light paved his path. He just had to point it in the right direction. Although the lantern let him only see six feet ahead, he saw another six feet with every step.

As we walk, we can see more of the road up ahead. This important part of visualization is more than seeing where we want to be. It is seeing how to get there. Having vision is seeing where to be. Visualization is seeing down the road that gets you there.

We don't visualize when we sit on our backsides and do nothing. Michael Angelo erected the statue of David from a large rock. He saw something in that large rock that no one else saw. Through

29

diligent work, patience and time he turned that rock into one of the most historic monuments ever erected. How did he see what no one else could? For years people would walk by the rock and think nothing of it, yet people now come from all over the world to see it. Michael used his visualization skills and saw the statue before any one else could. That's the type of foresight that exists in a peak performer.

I'm not talking about tunnel vision. Those with tunnel vision see only what lies before them. Those with a vision for what their minds can conceive are real visionaries. You not only believe, you realize you can conceive and thereby achieve. I have always been of the philosophy that if I can see it, only time stands in the way of me accomplishing it. You have to learn to be a power thinker. You have to learn to see where no man can see.

I'm not talking about pipe dreams. I'm talking about positive realistic visions that are reality in your mind. Thousands of years ago a boy named David became an achiever, the peak performer of peak performers. He achieved greatness and eventually became a king. His greatness didn't come because he was great. It came because his heart was in the right place. When everyone else ran scared he, a boy in statue confronted a giant and killed him. When he was needed to serve as king he did so with such greatness that he went down in the historic pages of the Bible itself.

Do you believe that David had vision or do you believe he just woke up one day and said I think I'll be king today! I believe you will agree that David had a vivid vision to see beyond the physical into the spiritual world. Helen Keller was once asked what would be worse than being blind. She answered, "To have sight and no vision." Keeping your eyes focused in the right direction gives meaning to your vision.

People loose sight of what they desire in life only to become a dreamer. There is a big difference between dreaming and being a dreamer. Dreamers dream about one thing one day and another thing the next. They talk a good talk but walk a poor walk. True peak performers are visionaries. They see beyond what today holds. Sacrifices are accepted as a means of achieving their specific dream.

A good example of a visionary in the hotel business would be J. Willard Marriott. He saw what tomorrow held and adapted to it before he had to. Visionaries see what tomorrow holds before tomorrow comes. They make things happen by seeing what is necessary long before most do and leading others in the right direction. They also do not have a problem admitting when they are wrong. They have a zeal that catches. Those around them catch the vision. They have no problem seeing the ultimate goal.

To have dreams in life means we must have hope. Hope for today. Hope for tomorrow. Hope for us. Hope for our loved ones. Hope for eternity. Hope that lasts forever.

How do you find hope? What makes us happy? Is it love? Peace of mind? I believe that it's a combination of all of these things and more. In my book *True Prosperity: Achieving Success in a World of Failure,* I spoke about how you find true hope in life. It begins with your relationship with God, then your family and lastly others.

The art of visualization is simple yet complex. Its simplicity lies within the fact that seeing things doesn't require an accumulation of education. The complexity lies in knowing which things to focus your efforts instead of things that only distract. Often people concentrate on things of little significance.

Oliver Wendell Holmes once said, "Man's mind, once stretched by a new idea, never regains its original dimensions." If peak performance is something you are striving for, realize this important fact. If you are of the millions of thoughtless talkers or wishers and would like to change, you can. But first you must know what you want. Visualization requires focusing your mind on what you desire. It is realizing this is something I can do. It may take God's help, or someone else's. It may require resources. But you visualize the path towards the vision. The steps that get you there become the plan. Many people don't take the first step because they don't see how to get there. They assume it is impossible. Visualization performs the miracle that allows your mind to believe it can happen. It bewilders me that a person can talk about believing in God yet not believe in the infinite wisdom He placed within each and every one of us.

Allow me to make another observation. There is an ever-increasing school of thought that argues that we are gods. Beware of this eastern teaching of deceit. I know three things for sure. There is a God, it isn't me and it isn't you either! Theodore Roosevelt once said, "Keep your eyes on the stars and your feet on the ground." Very wise words when it comes to realizing who you are, where you are going and where you came from.

An important part of becoming a peak performer is what I call the *Humble Factor*—no pun intended! If you are to tap down within yourself and follow the recommendations of this book yet forget this concept, it would all be in vain. One of the greatest destroyers of dreams today is pride. Solomon wrote in the book of Proverbs that pride leads to destruction and humility leads to honor. Those words of wisdom can't be overemphasized. I have seen countless others reach the pinnacle of success only to throw it all away over pride. Do what you do because it's the right thing to do, not to impress others. Many people buy things they do not want with money they do not have to impress people they do not like!

Have you ever stopped to wonder why that is? The answer is pride, and the solution is humility. It is not a lack of confidence, self-esteem or worthiness but genuine humility from the heart. Wear your armor as David did. He wore his not someone else's. You know the end result. He won! Eric Buttterworth once said, "You are not what you are but rather what you can be." Be yourself.

There are three distinct types of individuals that Robert Schuller talks about in his writings. The first is the "I-I" person. The I-I people are interested in themselves. No matter what the subject matter, the I-I person wants to know what's in it for them. When they visualize their life they do so in a way that leaves others out of the result. The next type of person is the "I-it" person. The I-it person is interested in materialistic possessions. The kind of car the I-it person drives may be more important than the school his children attend. The I-it person cares what others have to say about the house he lives in, the clothes he wears and the lifestyle revolving around his possessions.

The last of these types is the "I-you" person. The I-you person cares about others and as he visualizes his destiny, he includes them in his plans. If I could motivate you to become one of those people, it would be the I-you person. I have yet to find one I-you person that regrets that choice. I have seen the other types that live a miserable life. It's important that you realize the importance of being an I-you person.

Remember, "The stars shine brightest when it's the darkest." Be a star and shine in a world of darkness. Visualize where you desire to be in your life, and be careful what you ask for. It is possible to obtain things that will wreck your life and the happiness of those around you. You can have what you want, but you must take all that goes with it.

Therefore, plan for that which you are sure will give to you, and those you care for, the greatest good here on earth. Pave the way for others to find hope.

CHANGE YOURSELF

35

STRATEGY 3 : AFFIRM YOUR PASSION

Fall in love with your work and never work another day in your life. That statement has been said among many great speakers. Although the word *love* may be used out of context, the implication here centers on enjoying what you do for a living. I always stress to all I consult the overriding need to create a passion for their work. Excellence comes from passion for what you do.

Webster's 21st Century Dictionary defines passion as strong feeling or emotion. Unfortunately, many have stronger feelings for the weekend than the time spent during the week. They have little passion for their job. Peak performers have passion for what they do. There is no comparison between a person that dreads going to work each day and one who strongly cares about the quality of what they produce.

"Whatever your hand finds to do, do it with all your might" (Ecclesiastes 9:10). Passion is synonymous with excellence. Vince Lombardi once said, "There is only one way to succeed in anything, and that is to give it everything." To pursue passion is to develop the foundations of excellence. These proven foundations remain the building blocks of all striving for peak performance in their life. Below are three building blocks proven true by countless experiences.

Quality
Quality is never an accident. Most businesses these days do not place emphasis on the quality of their work. The majority of people working for them are time tellers instead of clock builders. If you are interested in developing a successful lifestyle and work ethic you must have a team of clock builders. How do you do that?

First, make perfection your goal. Strive to do everything as if it were the last time you were going to be able to do it.

Next, make things simple. Albert Einstein once said, "Everything should be as simple as possible, but not simpler." People try to complicate things to the point of total confusion. Realize that the simple things are put here for the wise man to see. Wise up and look for simplicity in everything you do.

Last, be aware of the details. Countless, unseen details are the only difference between mediocrity and magnificence. By being detail oriented we become more aware of our work and focused on the outcome. When this happens we stroll the path to achieving excellence.

Good is never *good enough*. Good things only happen when planned. Bad things happen on their own. You have to plan quality in your life. Hold yourself responsible for higher standards than others expect from you. Realize that many times the difference between failure and success is doing something nearly right or doing it exactly right. Ask yourself, If I haven't got time to do it right, when will I find the time to do it over?

Service

People are not dependent on us; we are dependent on them. This statement should be written on the walls of every business in America. Tragically, an attitude ravages through businesses large and small. We are doing our customers a favor by serving them.

Successful businesses realize just the opposite. Our customers are doing us a favor by giving us the opportunity to serve them. Such a simple concept too often overlooked. Consequently service suffers. To perform at your peak make customer service a keyword in your plan.

According to the Nordstrom Employee Manual, the number one golden rule of service is as follows: "Use your good judgment in all situations. There are no additional rules. Remember that people don't care how much you know until they know how much you care."

Teamwork

There is a story about a man that got his car stuck while driving down a country road. He walked for quite a distance before coming to an old farmhouse. After knocking on the door an elderly man answered. "I seem to have gotten my car stuck up the road. Do you have a way of pulling me out?" asked the man. The elderly man answered calmly, "All I have is my old mule, Dusty. I'll hitch him up and see if I can help."

He hitched the mule up and proceeded to hook up to the man's automobile. "Go Charlie!" he exclaimed. Nothing happened. "Go Billy!" still nothing. "Go Dusty!" Finally Dusty begin to move.

After pulling out the car, the man asked the elderly man, "Why did you call your mule those two other names? The old man replied, "You know, Dusty is getting old and a little hard of hearing. If he knew he was pulling that car all by himself he may not have put forth any effort at all!"

That story holds a strong message concerning teamwork. Working together is the very essence of the excellence that results in peak performance. I once heard that a hurricane is defined as many raindrops cooperating. As long as they cooperate toward a goal that is for the good of the group, that definition probably rings true. No one person can accomplish anything great. It takes people working together toward a common goal. Regardless of how much money a company or individual makes, it does not happen alone. You alone cannot be the best at everything. But when you combine your talents, you can be the best at virtually anything. This requires the ability to build an effective team. Even this is worthless without the ability to play on that team.

No one can excuse themselves from this principle. Everyone operates on a team. The self-employed must cooperate with the customer to work the deal, the vendor to get the supplies needed. Even the boss is required to work with her employees to make a profit. Without effective teamwork the business will fail.

An effective team needs the following components:
1. Proper communication
2. Establishment of goals together
3. Focus
4. An open mind to progressive change
5. The willingness to confront failure with a winning attitude

Proper Communication is essential to any endeavor. Without the understanding based on effective communication, team members' efforts are not coordinated. They cease being a team as they go in their own direction. Goals are required to be discussed.

Establishment of Goals Together insures the team is communicating. It also gives ownership to each member. They will take more initiative to achieving objectives. Success will be the focus.

Focus on a single object, meeting the team's goal, keeps the team moving. The disorganization from not having properly communicated goals defeats the group's focus. Without focus the team loses motivation.

An open mind to progressive change requires commitment to meeting the team's goals. Without motivation to change, it likely will not occur. The incentive is the team's desire to achieve.

The willingness to confront failure with a winning attitude allows the team to reassess unrealistic goals. The team will not stall when encountering obstacles.

It's been said that no one can whistle a symphony. It takes an orchestra to play it. A good rule of thumb for teamwork is to involve everyone in everything. Henry Ford once said, "Coming together is a beginning. Keeping together is progress. Working together is success." Teamwork is the ability to work toward a common vision. It is the fuel that allows common people to attain uncommon results. The object is not to see through one another, but to see each other through.

I challenge you to begin looking closely at those that have attained success of a great nature in their life. In other words, the ones you would classify as peak performers. The overwhelming odds, magnificent feats and determination not to quit lead them to greatness. The Rev. Billy Graham, Henry Ford, Thomas Edison, Albert Einstein, Alexander Graham Bell, W. Clement Stone, The Apostle Paul. All of these men had one thing in common. They all had passion. Their pursuit of success was much more than that of money. It was the challenge. It was the satisfaction of the achievement. It was passion.

All who have a real passion for peak performance have a mission. They set their sights on a target and hit it. Peak performers also need to have a purpose. A purpose is a personal, long-term affirmation of what you want "to be." It offers direction to your life. The guiding principal may be a line from a song, an inspirational quote, a Scripture verse or anything else that establishes the tone for your statement.

There are people that have lost their wealth in pursuit of their dream. Although loosing everything is not what we are advocating, these people have a hunger. A hunger that makes them consider taking a loss to eventually win. A burning desire to succeed overrides their fear of risk.

In order to restrain from pursuing some unrealistic fantasy, we remain focused with our passion. Anyone can lay down everything running after what they should not. Few can remain focused on their dreams without being distracted. Passionate people need to grasp the difference between reality and wild ideas.

So how do you obtain passion if you do not possess it? What is the secret to a passionate heart and a driving spirit? The answer quite simply is attitude. Attitude determines where we are in life and where we are going.

If you are a pilot, you are familiar with the *artificial horizon,* the gauge that determines your attitude. It explains the relationship of the aircraft to the horizon. If you change the position of the aircraft you change its performance. Our lives are much like that of an aircraft. If we change our position or outlook on certain things we change our performance.

If we are to perform at our peak, we have to change how we view things. The attitude you possess toward life and your work is totally up to you. You are responsible for how you feel about something. Your success in life is caused more by mental attitude than by mere mental capacity. The Stanford Research Institute says that the money you make in any endeavor is determined by 13 percent of knowledge and 87 percent by your ability to deal with people. J. Paul Getty when asked what was the most important quality for a successful executive replied, "It doesn't make much difference how much other knowledge or experience a person possesses, if he is

41

unable to achieve results through people, he is worthless as an executive."

People who rise to the top have a good attitude. They do not get there by hoping, wishing or thinking. It's been said that your attitude determines your altitude in life. Truer words could not be spoken. Peak performers understand the principal behind attitude and ultimately passion. They strive to look at the world through different glasses than most.

John Maxwell in his book, *The Winning Attitude* discussed a study done by Telemetrix International. The study concerned those "nice guys" that climbed the corporate ladder. A total of 16,000 executives were studied. The study revealed that high achievers (peak performers) tended to care about people as well as profits whereas low achievers were preoccupied with their own security. High achievers viewed subordinates optimistically; low achievers showed a basic distrust of subordinates' abilities. High achievers sought advice from their subordinates, but low achievers did not. High achievers were listeners; low achievers avoided communication and relied on policy manuals. This study reveals what peak performers have known all along. To be a top achiever you must have passion, and to have passion you must have a good attitude. If we are to be peak performers we cannot minimize the importance of a healthy attitude. We become overly concerned with believing intelligence equals success. Although intelligence is an important quality, it pales in comparison to attitude.

A certain university alumni association official observed how attitude makes the difference in the life of a student. He informed others at the university to always be kind to you're A and B students. Someday one of then will return to your campus as a good professor. By the same token you should be kind to your B and C students. Someday one of them will return and build a two million-dollar science laboratory. In essence, their attitude determines their altitude in life.

Your attitude at the beginning of a task will determine the outcome. Preparation is an essential to a peak performer aimed at making it happen in his or her life. Having a positive yet realistic view at the task set out before us increases our odds greatly of achieving our goals.

If I had to summarize what passion is and is not, I would do so as follows:

Passion is:
1. Working for the enjoyment and challenge it brings
2. Being a positive realist
3. Striving for peak performance at all you do

Passion is not:
1. Working only for the money it brings
2. Being a positive dreamer
3. Striving for peak performance (what can I get out of it or what's in it for me)

I realize that for many working for the shear enjoyment of it sounds a little crazy. Granted that we all must be compensated for our performance; however, what is the quality of life if that is your soul purpose? If you were scheduled for brain surgery how comforting would it be to know that he was doing it only for the money? Should the physician be paid well for his service? Absolutely. Should that be all that is on his mind? Absolutely not!

Realizing the importance of a realistic positive outlook is equally important. I can look at a flowerbed full of weeds. But simply saying they're not there won't make them go away. On the other hand seeing the weeds, I realize to keep them from overtaking the flowers I must remove them.

We allow the life to be taken out of us when we pursue a venture dying before our eyes. Blinded by unrealistic expectations we fall short of our goals. Often pride, misunderstanding and a lack of wisdom guide us.

The purpose of this book is to get you to make a commitment to make things happen. Anyone can work on a project. Very few have the ambition and drive to *make it happen*. That's why I chose that as the title of this book. Making things happen is a rare talent, but it is something you can learn.

You can have passion in your life. You can possess the attitude that translates into winning. You can make it happen in your life.

If you do not have the passion you desire, make a decision now to change. Read and re-read strategy one. Make passion an integral part of you life by creating the right attitude. Before continuing to strategy four, decide to make this strategy a reality. Ask yourself this important question. If I was independently wealthy, would I continue doing what I am doing or would I do something else. The answer will reveal the truth concerning your passion for your career and your life.

CHANGE YOURSELF

45

STRATEGY 4 : NEVER, NEVER QUIT

During the darkest days of Great Britain's history, one man helped hold the nation together with his bulldogged tenacity. He refused to quit no matter how stiff the opposition. His resolve to continue was forged not in the crucible of war but in grade school.

Legend has it that young Winston Churchill tried three times to pass the final exam at Harrow in Brighton, England. He didn't give up then, and fifty years later he reminded a nation to do the same. In late October of 1941 during World War II, Churchill agreed to address his alma mater. The school had just been fire bombed.

The Prime Minister ascended the lectern in the speech room where he must have sat in hundreds of times before in his youth. His message was simple. His words must have rung with the clarity of meaning burned in his mind from the persistence he learned so long ago.

> Never give in—never, never, never, never, in
> nothing great or small, large or petty, never give
> in except to convictions of honour and good
> sense. Never yield to force; never yield to the
> apparently overwhelming might of the enemy.

Proverbs 21:5 reminds us that steady plotting brings prosperity. Persistence and determination are at the very core of success achievement in an individual's life. We have been concentrating on foundational strategies that allow us to attain peak performance, making things happen in life. Although these strategies are designed to do just that, strategy four is the bridge between just thinking about it and actually doing it.

The fear of failure causes people to give up before reaching their prize in life. It intimidates you, and stands in your way. Such pitfalls line the winning path to catch the losers. Only those keeping their eye on the prize will reach their goal. I have, more times than I wish to remember, pursued a goal only to fail.

Failure is an event, not a person. It doesn't have to be a destination. Accept the fact that you are a winner and act that way. Realize where your power and strength comes from. Then you will ultimately receive the prize. Dr. Joyce Brothers once said, "You can't perform in a manner that is inconsistent with the way you see yourself." If you see yourself fat, you will be fat. If you see yourself dumb, odds are others will see you that way. The next time you look in the mirror ask yourself what you see. The answer will go a long way towards telling why you have or haven't performed at the level you are capable of.

It often takes years to see the effects of a winning attitude. The story of the ancient bamboo tree illustrates my point. The Chinese bamboo tree hardly grows until its fifth year. The first year it must be cared for but nothing is shown for it. The second year is the same. The third and forth years are no different. Finally the fifth year the plant grows 90 feet in only six weeks of time. It doesn't grow one inch before that time, yet if it is not watered, nurtured and cared for, it will not grow when the time comes for it to sprout.

What are you striving for that could take more patience and persistence than the Chinese bamboo tree? Just because you cannot see the efforts of your work does not mean that it's going unnoticed or it will not pay off in the future. The only difference between one who wins and one who looses is the one who wins does not quit. Wellington who defeated Napoleon at Waterloo was asked why the British army was so successful. His reply was because they had trained to always fight for an additional five minutes longer than everyone else had.

A man in a restaurant once noticed a woman that continued to look at him to the point of staring. After a period of time the man asked her if something was wrong.

"You look just like my third husband. Your eyes, the clothes you wear, everything about you looks like my third husband."

"How many times have you been married?"

"Twice."

That's determination. Be determined and take pride in everything you do.

There is a story about a builder and a carpenter in which the carpenter did not take pride in his work. An elderly carpenter was ready to retire. He told his employer-contractor of his plans to leave the house building business and live a more leisurely life with his wife. He would miss the paycheck, but he needed to retire. They could get by. The contractor was sorry to see his good worker go and asked if he could build just one more house as a personal favor. The carpenter said yes, but in time it was easy to see his heart was not in his work. He resorted to poor workmanship and used inferior materials. It was an unfortunate way to end his career. When the carpenter finished his work and the builder came to inspect the house, the contractor handed the front door key to the carpenter. "This is your house," he said, "my gift to you."

What a shock! What a shame! If only he had known he was building his own house. He would have done it so differently. Now he had to live in the house he built none too well. So it is with our lives. We are willing to put up with less than the best. At crucial points we do not give the job our best effort. Faced with the situation we just created, we realize we're living in the house we ourselves have built. We've made our beds. Now we must lie in them. If we had only realized, we would have done it differently.

Think of yourself as the carpenter. Think about your house. Each day you hammer a nail, place a board, or erect a wall. Build wisely. It is the only life you will ever build. Even if you live it for only one day more, that day deserves to be lived to its fullest, with no regrets. The plaque on your wall should say, "Life is a do-it-yourself project."

Who could say it more clearly? Your life is the result of your attitudes and choices in the past. Your life tomorrow will be the result of your attitudes and the choices you make today. You are already a winner. In Beaumont, Texas at the turn of the century a man was asked if a drilling company could drill for oil on his land. After granted permission oil was found and it proved to be one of the largest oil strikes of its time known as Spindle Top. The question I have for you is simple. Was this man a millionaire before or after they struck oil on his property? He was a millionaire all along. However, until you recognize, confess, accept and develop you may as well not have. Persistence is much the same way. If we are to ever reach our goals in life we must accept the fact that they have already been reached. Everybody else just can't see it yet.

Some of you may be thinking that it is too late. You are too old or that it won't work anymore. How do you know it won't work if you don't make an effort?

What would you do if you knew you could not fail? What would you be doing today? Is it the same as what you are doing? We all would probably make some changes.

Failure is an event not a destination. All of us will occasionally fail on our climb upwards. Whether we remain down or get back up is completely up to us. Don't allow a crisis to become a ruin. Turn your obstacles into opportunities.

Begin sewing good actions. It goes like this.

• Sew an action—reap a habit
• Sew a habit—reap a character
• Sew a character—reap a destiny

Stay determined in all you do. Realize you may not make the right decisions all the time. That's okay. Winners don't always make the right decisions; they just persist to make the decisions they make right.

An oak tree is nothing more than a little nut that never gave up it's ground. Success comes to those that pursue it one inch at a time. Oliver Wendell Holmes said, "The greatest thing in the world is not so much where we are, but rather in what direction we are moving." The apostle Paul once wrote in the book of Philippians, "Forgetting what is behind us and straining toward what is ahead, I press on toward the goal" (3:13–14).

No, it's not too late, nor is the world made up of lucky individuals. Luck has been defined as *Labor Under Concentrated Knowledge*. It's also never too early to start your drive and mission in life. Mozart was only seven when he published his first musical composition. George Bernard Shaw produced an award winning play when he was 94 years of age. Benjamin Franklin helped fame the constitution when he was 81 years of age. Brent Vogle was 41 when he completed a sanctioned 26.2-mile marathon. The question you must ask yourself is how old would you be if you didn't know how old you were? The fact is it doesn't matter when you do something great. Age has little to do with ability.

We want, want, and want, but we are not willing to pay the price to get it. Persistence and determination are the keys to never quitting. There may come a time that we have to change course because we are headed down the wrong path. In these cases we have to develop our "know" muscles, our wisdom to do the right things. Many people fail by quitting too early. Countless stories throughout history tell of people who struck gold, oil, found treasures, built empires and the like against overwhelming odds. They could have quit, but something made them keep at it.

An aircraft is off course most of the time from one destination to the other; however, by making slight adjustments they arrive and no one knows the difference. The pilot is not unrealistic by thinking he can fly in any direction and arrive where he wishes. He charts his course and plans his journey, making corrections when needed.

Life is much the same. We must chart our course and plan our journey. We must never let go of our dreams and ambitions. An anonymous poem summarizes the importance of never giving up. The poem is titled "I'll Never Let Go."

I'll Never Let Go

I want to let go,
But I won't let go,
There are battles to fight by day and by night
And I'll never let go.
I'm sick and blue
And worried through and through
But I won't let go.
I won't let go,
But I won't let go.
I will never yield.
What lie down in the field and surrender my shield?
No! I'll never let go.

51

> I want to let go but I won't let go.
> May this be my song against legions of wrong
> Oh God keep me strong
> And I'll never let go.

Keep your eyes focused on that which you are striving for. There will always be those that will discourage you and tell you that you can't make it. Mountains will arise. Storms will come. Those that look past these things and learn from their mistakes will prosper.

The people you associate with have a big influence on your performance and your future. Choose your friends wisely. Regardless of how easy it may be to quit, vow to yourself not to be a statistic. Not everyone is made to be a leader of a major corporation. As you strive to be all you can, realize that you are a unique individual. No one in the world is just like you. Whatever your talent may be, be the best at it that you are capable of being.

Where so many fail is not just on the climb up but once they have reached the top. Although there is always room for improvement most become depressed when they reached their goals. They believed that something would change, that they would somehow feel a sense of eternal satisfaction. The truth of the matter is that these things are only temporary. If you are not happy with yourself, you will never be happy with any level of accomplishment.

True, money does not buy happiness. By the same token, it does not buy unhappiness either. No earthly possession ever will. Contentment comes from within. Your relationship with God, your family and others is all that will bring that type of lasting happiness so many are looking for.

I'm not to preach to you but rather to keep you moving in the right direction. Nothing is more tragic than one who accomplishes great things at the hands of overwhelming odds and throws it all away because it wasn't what he was looking for.

CHANGE YOURSELF

53

STRATEGY 5 : GET FOCUSED

An old Chinese proverb advises that the longest journey begins with the first step. But in which direction do we take that first step in becoming a peak performer?

In his classic "Sea Ballads" John Masefield wrote, "All I ask is for a tall ship and a star to steer her by." Ancient mariners would stand behind the wheel and focus on a single star. Steering by that star would take them to their destination.

This is the basis of focus. Know where you want to go. Plan your success. Find out how to get there. Then focus on it; make it the star you steer by.

Focus brings clarity. It filters out the less important. It separates the good from the great allowing us to concentrate on achieving the latter.

Distraction is one of the deadly killers of success in the world today. We are surrounded with more opportunities today than ever before. The problem arises when we do not keep our eyes focused on the target that we are aiming for. In my book titled, *True Prosperity*, I discussed the four *D*s of destruction that we are faced with in life. Regardless of who you are, constant distraction seems to be the rule rather than the exception.

Willie was a man that had great talent. He had vision and the ability to carry it through. He was an inspiration to me when I first started my business. No matter what I needed he was always there. To be quite honest, I thought he was one the greatest business minds in his profession. People would come from all over to see what he was doing. As time went on he would call me with what sounded like great business ventures. Some I would express an interest in and others I would not. Eventually something happened. Willie became more interested in new ideas than in remembering what brought him success through the years. He moved outside of his talent, of what he was designed to do.

Hardly a week would go by that he didn't call me with another idea. After a period of time his dreams became unrealistic. They would include the moon and the stars. Unrealistic ventures were presented that would bring a million dollars in just a few days, yet I never saw any of them materialize into anything more than disappointment. I began to question him extensively about each idea, but he always seemed to have a quick answer. His businesses suffered. Ultimately he had little to show for his efforts. He became terminally ill with cancer, and eventually passed on. I couldn't help but wonder what he could have accomplished with his life if he would have just stayed focused. Although some of the deals he had may have panned out, how much more could he have done if he would have understood the principal behind distraction?

Distraction encroaches silently. In an instant focus is lost. Once distracted, your sense of direction fools you. You are certain what you're chasing deserves your attention. It is bound to pay off. But you are being set up. Distraction allows the next stage, deceit to quickly set in. It falsely comforts providing all the answers. It reasons and justifies with you that you are on the right path. When this happens to you it is imperative that you develop your sense of listening to the voice inside of you. Regardless of how it may look on the outside, learn to listen. Be concerned if you don't see a downside to a plan. Being prepared if things should not work out is wisdom at its best form.

The next stage after deceit is defeat. When we are distracted and led into deceit we generally are not aware of what is happening. Defeat setting in is the first step in realizing that we have made the wrong choice. It is during this stage that we see the empty pot at the end of the rainbow. We can finally see all the wrong things begin to surface. Defeat is a humbling experience. It takes no preference on whom it strikes. Those with prideful hearts are struck the hardest. I know. I was one of them. The worse thing about defeat is that it ultimately leads to destruction, the final stage of distraction.

Loose your focus and this is where you're heading. The destruction stage of distraction is the bottom of the pit. Avoid it. There is no mercy here for those failing to recognize they've taken the wrong path.

To avoid these progressive stages, be aware of your surroundings and those you come in contact with. Be willing to admit you made a mistake. Don't commit yourself to operating from a bad position. Make whatever changes are necessary. Many take the downward spiral simply because than they are not willing to admit they are wrong. They allow pride to destroy their lives rather than acknowledge their mistake. On the surface it all seems so simple. However, if you believe it won't happen to you, you've just taken the first step in the cycle.

The secret to an effective life is focus. It is the very key to peak performance in life. Without it you will drift through life ending up wherever life takes you. Most that allow this to happen to them do not achieve any of their life's ambitions and blame the world for their heartache. Proverbs 4:25 says, "Keep your eyes on what is right, and look ahead to what is good." To make something happen in your life without focusing your attention is like throwing a basketball around a court, expecting it to land in the goal every time. Vision allows you to see what lies ahead for you if you are persistent. Focus is the fuel that gets you there. You have probably seen movies depicting oriental culture that speak of focus. Often these films deal with martial arts and training. Frequently you will hear the word focus used.

I once heard a story concerning someone who had driven a racecar in a training session with an instructor. The instructor informed him to keep his eyes where he wanted to go not where he was going. After circling the track several times the instructor, having special controls on his side of the car, used them to place the car into a spin. Startled by the car being out of control the driver began to panic. Immediately the instructor pointed at the road exclaiming, "Look where you want to go not where you are going." The driver looked where he wanted to go and he gained control of the car. Again, after several laps the instructor placed the car in a spin. Startled again he began looking where he was headed instead of where he wanted to go. The instructor repeated the same words telling him to look where he wants to go not where he is going. Finally the driver gained control of the automobile and maintained it the rest of the time.

What lesson is there to be learned from this story? Success in life involves focusing on a target. We have a choice of focusing on where we want to go or looking in all different directions believing that sooner or later we will get there. Nothing could be further from the truth. Focus means just that. We must look straight ahead, piercing though anything that stands in our way. Nothing can distract us. Nothing can divert our attention. The world may try to tear you apart. If you keep your eye on target, they won't beat you. Keep your focus.

To be focused means having an idea where you're heading. Our eyes are looking in the direction we want to go with no diversion. When we look through binoculars we must first focus the lens before we can see with any clarity. So also do we focus on where we want to go in life.

To keep from becoming distracted ask yourself these simple questions.

- Is (whatever it may be) going to make a difference 5, 10 or even 20 years from now?
- Is pursuing this to reality in my best interests and of those closest to me?
- When realized will I feel a sense of accomplishment, satisfied that no one was harmed in the process?

If you can truthfully answer yes to these questions, then odds are it's worth focusing on. Today most businesses admit they often lose focus. "Let's get back to the basics" is a common slogan among leaders. The world is full of distractions and temptations. Often people change directions more often than they changed majors in college. They commit to a winning objective only to have something catch their eye. Like a dog chasing a car, they run after another opportunity, losing their focus along the way.

The most successful companies focus on very few things. Consider Microsoft. What do they do? It isn't hard to figure out. Bill Gates has placed all of his energy into developing the best software available. It also goes without saying that he isn't doing it for the money. He has already made more than anyone else. It is his passion. He does it because he enjoys it and is committed to quality.

Before you begin to duplicate your efforts in another area you should be successful in one. I have watched many people never reach the pinnacle of success because they branch off into another area. Remember, anything with more than one vision creates division. If you are going to make things happen, have a focused vision that sees things others will not see.

If I could tell a person striving to perform at their peak one thing, it would be to remain focused on your vision and mission. Allow people to be themselves by working within their own fingerprints, their own uniquely individual pattern. You will encounter the most difficulty managing deadlines. Getting people to complete projects by a certain time plagues managers. Keeping everyone focus is key.

No matter the length of time in business, you will encounter struggles with staying on a target. A person pitches a hot idea. It must be jumped at now or it's gone. Consider passing on it if it vies for your focus. After reaching a point of success and you have the time to fully consider other possibilities to increase your profitability, you can afford to go for it, but not before.

When people tempt you, keep striving. When they make fun of you, keep striving. When no one believes in you, keep striving. Put yourself in the categories with the great ones, those that kept the vision and never gave up. By doing so you will be one of the few that possess the ability to make things happen.

Below are a few summarizations concerning what focus is and is not:

FOCUS IS:
1. Understanding what your vision and mission is.
2. Committing to your vision and mission.
3. Seeing that those around you that are assisting you in your mission understand numbers 1 and 2.
4. Being known for something specific and great.

FOCUS IS NOT:
1. Believing a vision and mission statement is something that looks pretty on paper and belongs there rather than in the heart.
2. Jumping on every "opportunity" that comes our way
3. Not considering the effects of our actions on others but rather what could be in it for us.
4. Being known for many things but none that are excellent.

As you strive for excellence you will increasingly realize the importance of remaining focused. I once saw a definition of success that I thought would do well for focus. It is the progressive realization of a worthy idea. Commit to focus by completing the form below.

Commitment to Focus Statement:

I _____, do hereby commit to my vision and mission in life. I will do all I can to see that I stand for excellence and whatever I do it will be done to the best of my God given abilities.

_____
Your signature

CHANGE YOURSELF

61

STRATEGY 6 : EARN RESPECT BY EXEMPLIFYING LEADERSHIP

Respect seldom finds its way into many conversations today. It is absent altogether from contemporary vocabulary. Rarer still are the times respect plays itself out in relationships.

Why has respect fallen out of style? Primarily respect's demise comes at the hand of a general lack of character. A perceived lack of value in another breeds disrespect. A person feeling unvalued will not give you respect.

Tragically many in leadership do not respect those under them. It takes no special qualifications to place demands on people. Regardless of skill, anyone can be a belligerent supervisor. Not just anyone, however, can influence a group, inspiring them to carry out your goals.

You may know someone like that. It's the sign of a good leader. If you desire respect from others, give it first without expectations in return. Peak performers respect the needs and beliefs of those they come in contact with. Once the respect level has been established the people in question must be able to see true character in all of your actions. It must be the real thing or else the respect you are working for will never manifest. The Rodney Dangerfield syndrome of "I don't get no respect" doesn't go very far in the real world. To get respect, as this strategy suggests, we have to earn it.

The most dangerous creature on earth is not a roaring lion or a hungry grizzly bear. It is a man with a microphone. The saddest are the people whom that man entices down the wrong path. History is replete with stories of people led through blind faith directly to their graves.

Realize there is a difference between blind faith and respect. A leader should set out to gain the respect of others by living an open life for the entire world to see. True respect comes no other way. The best way to describe respect is to relate it to leadership. For the sake of this strategy we will discuss the fundamentals of leadership and how they relate to respect.

Developing respect requires learning how to function as an effective leader. First let's clarify one important issue. You can be a leader without being a peak performer, but you can't be a peak performer without being a leader. True leaders, the ones we will be discussing in this strategy, are peak performers driven to completing tasks with excellence and on time.

Leaders constantly clarify their goals and missions. They elevate, motivate and celebrate with their teams. An example of this would be the quarterback on a football team. He may be their leader, but he has to also become one of them. He cannot "lord" over them. This doesn't build respect. He calls the plays and is responsible for the outcome, but he realizes that it takes everyone to make things happen.

Requirements of Leadership

The number one requirement of a leader is credibility. If you say you are going to do something, you must carry it through. You must be on time for appointments. You must show up. People have to see the fact that what you say is what you mean and you will carry it through.

If I say that I will see you at a certain place and time and do not show up, I loose a portion of credibility. If it happens on a regular occasion, I loose all of my credibility.

Financial institutions rely on credit reports to give them an indication of what kind of person you are. If you pay your bills on time, you are credible. If not, you are not.

The second requirement of leaders is character. This is a subject that you cannot discuss enough. *Webster's 7ᵗʰ Edition New Collegiate Dictionary* defines character as

> 1. One of the attributes or features that make and distinguish the individual. 2. Reputation. 3. Moral excellence and firmness.

One of the foundational cornerstones of success in life or in any venture is possessing character. Integrity and backbone are the standards of this great quality. Character should not be confused with having character. One can be a character and have no character at all.

Furthermore, not all leaders have character. We are discussing peak performers. All peak performers possess character. There are many world-renowned leaders that had no character or morals at all. Without naming names you can probably make a list yourself. Today's youth grow up—with few exceptions—without the benefit of role modes with any character. Addiction, violence and immorality now characterize pro sports, once full of examples for the young.

Abraham Lincoln speaking of character said, "Fame is a vapor. Popularity, an accident. Riches take wings. People who cheer you today will curse you tomorrow. One thing only endures, and that is character."

The last fundamental requirement of leadership is humility. Maintain an attitude of gratitude. Pride only leads to destruction in life. Arrogance kills more dreams than anything else. There is nothing wrong with a healthy pride through a high self-esteem. Being proud of your accomplishments, taking pride in the way you dress, the way you present yourself, is only healthy and builds up our self-image. On the other hand, becoming arrogant is detrimental.

It amazes me what people will do for the sheer sake of being right. This only feeds the ego. It does not earn respect. Successful leaders realize that loosing makes an opportunity for winning the next time. Being wrong this time makes it possible to be right. When we understand these principals the sky becomes the limit to what we can accomplish. Who cares who receives the credit for success as long as the whole team gets there?

Don't confuse the ego-feeding obsession to be perceived as being right with having principles that allow you to do right. There are times that an individual must stand up for what is right. The way to realize if something is worth it, however, is to ask ourselves an important question: What difference will this issue make in the scheme of eternity? Consider this when mired in minor issues. True leaders live with an eternal perspective.

One of the funniest persons ever to live, Erma Bombeck, had the ability to make people laugh even when the situation called for tears. This gift was never more apparent than when the nation observed the humorist's struggle with cancer. While battling for her life she wrote a column entitled "If I had My Life to Live Over." Answering her own question she shared, "I'd have cherished every moment [of her pregnancy] and realized that the wonderment growing inside me was the only chance in life to assist God in a miracle. Given another shot at life, I would seize every minute." At that point in her life Erma realized the importance of looking at things with an eternal view. Soon after, in 1996, she lost her battle with cancer.

Leaders are driven by a mission. We have talked about this in previous strategies, but its importance cannot be undervalued. Without a mission people have nothing to follow except a person. Respect has to be larger than the individual. It must encompass everything he or she stands for. Before leaders can lead others respectively, they must lead themselves.

In order to stress the points that create respect, we will now look at those things that will destroy your respect and ability as a leader. As we discuss each one, realize that avoiding these seven things enhances your ability to earn the respect necessary to become, or continue to be, a peak performer.

Seven Wounds That Will Destroy Your Ability as A Leader

Number One: Trying To Do Everything Yourself
You must learn how to delegate if you are going to be an effective leader. D. L. Moody once said, "I would rather put ten men to work than to do the work of ten men." In *Developing the Leader within You,* Dr. John Maxwell illustrates the futility of refusing to partner with others. Maxwell tells of a bricklayer who tried to move five hundred pounds of bricks from the top of a four-story building to the sidewalk below. People, who are placed in leadership positions, but attempt to do it alone, will someday come to the same conclusion he did.

His problem was that he tried to do it alone by lowering the bricks in a barrel with a rope. He soon found out that the barrel weighed more than he did. His shortsightedness in trying to do the work alone led to his flying through the air. Due to the subsequent injuries the man was required to fill out an insurance form. The last question on the form asked what he'd do different facing the same situation in the future. His response, "Please be advised that I am finished trying to **do the job alone.**"

Number Two: Stops Caring

A caring attitude is essential in developing respect and leading others. People need to know that you care about them and their performance. They need to know that they are more than a number or a statistic. They need to see the human side of you. In doing so you will create a mutual respect that will go a long way towards developing long lasting, productive relationships.

The major cause of the lack of employee loyalty is they don't think you care about them. This is especially true in the corporate environment. If they believe you care more about the bottom line, you will ever be looking over you shoulder instead of focusing up ahead.

Even outside the office, relationships feed off mutual respect and trust. If you project an uncaring attitude, you will receive the same in return. A person that feels cared for will be loyal, giving everything he has for you.

Number Three: Stops Growing

You can never stop learning. It is the basic foundation to becoming a peak performer and remaining one. A good illustration of this is the *parable of the black belt.*

Picture a martial artist kneeling before his teacher in a ceremony to receive his black belt. After years of persistence and training, the student has finally reached the pinnacle of achievement in the discipline. Then, just when the student thinks he has completed the journey he is told he must pass one more test.

The student says he is ready. The teacher says you must answer one essential question: "What is the true meaning of the black belt?" "The end of my journey," responds the student. "A well deserved reward for all of my hard work."

The teacher waits for more. Clearly he is not satisfied, so he tells the student he is not ready for the black belt. He tells the student to return in one year.

A year later the student returns this time more determined than ever. "What is the meaning of the black belt?" asks the teacher. "A symbol of high achievement and distinction in our art," says the student.

The teacher waits for more. "You are still not ready for the black belt," says the teacher. The student is instructed to return in one year.

A year later the student returns and kneels in front of the teacher. "What is the true meaning of the black belt," asks the teacher. The student responds, "The black belt is the beginning of knowledge, the state of a never-ending journey of discipline, work, and the pursuit of an ever higher standard," says the student. "Yes. You are now ready to receive the black belt and *begin* your journey," the teacher responds.

This story illustrates how important it is to realize that learning is a journey not a destination. Make learning a passion and set out on a journey that will lead to a land of knowledge and wisdom.

Number Four: Loses Touch with People

If you desire respect from others you need to stay in touch with them. Stay connected. Move towards your goals as a team, a unit. Disjointed team members loose contact and ultimately the shared vision. They begin doing their own thing. Make sure you regularly make contact, a phone call, an email, or a brief face-to-face conversation.

Always ask for feedback. What someone has to say may be the difference between success and failure for a company. That's because companies are made up of people, and people need to feel needed. Feedback is *the breakfast of champions.* Ask for it and you will be surprised what you will find out, not to mention the respect you will receive. Proverbs 20:18 says, "Don't charge into battle without a plan." Plan your success by including others in your vision.

Number Five: Becomes Complacent and Less Grateful
There is a big difference between complacency and contentment. Being complacent is lighting a match in a room filled with gas—only without knowing it. Young men are complacent, thinking they will be young and healthy forever. Complacency knows of risk and doesn't care. That is not the same as being a risk taker. Often peak performers are required to take risks. A complacent person is irresponsible regarding risk. A risk taker respects risk and tries to manage it.

Gratefulness goes right along with respect. Respect is shown through gratefulness. Always be grateful and learn to be a servant as well as a leader. Remember, the greatest and most respected leaders of all times were also servants. By remaining thankful for all you have you can prevent the next wound from taking place.

Number Six: Becomes Arrogant
Although we have discussed this point before, it is a wound that will prevent respect from coming your way in life. Dr. Joyce Brothers once said, "There is a rule in sailing where the more maneuverable ship should give way to the less maneuverable craft. I think this is sometimes a good rule to follow in human relations as well." Remain humble in all that you do. As we have stated earlier, humility is one of the key ingredients of a true peak performer.

Number Seven: Gets Distracted
As we discussed in Strategy Five, focus is the fuel that brings vision to reality. Remain purpose driven. Understand the stages of destruction that distraction can lead to. By realizing what is ahead you can prepare before you arrive.

Promote positive influence to all those you come in contact with. Exemplify honesty and integrity. Treat everyone, as you would want to be treated. That's the essence of leadership and that's the essence of respect.

Why is respect so hard to find in the world today? Simply because there are very few that possess the qualities of a true leader. The meekest of the many will sometimes be the greatest of the few. Set out to gain respect the old fashion way—and I might add, the only way—by *earning it.*

CHANGE YOURSELF
71

STRATEGY 7 : YEARN TO AWAKEN : AND RELEASE YOUR : POTENTIAL WITHIN

Inside each and every one of us lies a potential to do things greater than most of us can conceive. One of the differences between peak performers and underachievers is their ability to recognize and awaken this potential to become all we are capable of becoming. In order to recognize this in ourselves we need to first possess the yearning desire to do so. It is when we possess this desire that we can develop our mindset to become a power thinker.

Power thinkers think powerful thoughts, the kind that changes themselves and the world. They reach down inside themselves and find a part that they didn't realize existed. Think of this potential as you would diamonds deep within the walls of a mine. When you dig diligently without giving up you have the opportunity to find what lies below. To do so takes desire, persistence and the willingness to fail. To reach down and release this potential takes three things: visualization, determination and realization.

Visualization. In strategy two we discussed having a vision in detail. Power thinkers seem to be able to bring something out of nothing. They remain focused and unfold every cover that may lie over their God-given abilities. They create dreams by possessing hope. This hope allows them to continue their journey down the path to ultimate achievement. In essence, they believe in themselves so much that nothing will stand in the way of their desires. Their belief in themselves creates an overwhelming belief in those surrounding them because they know the potential within each individual.

That's what visualization is all about. If there is something you want out of life, you can make it a reality by *seeing it happen* in your mind over and over until it becomes a reality. I have taught my kids how to use visualization in their lives as well. For instance, before a ballgame I will make them close their eyes and see themselves hitting the ball until they feel they own that vision. Then we will visualize where the ball will go and them running around the bases.

This exercise, however silly it may sound, works and mentally prepares them for the game. Nothing mystical happens. You are giving yourself encouragement. The power is in allowing yourself the permission to succeed.

This same technique will work for you as well if you really concentrate and allow your mind to work at its highest capability. If there is something you desire to do with your life, use visualization to motivate you to succeed.

Determination. Anything significant accomplished by anyone requires determination. With determination comes the persistence to stand against overwhelming odds. Napoleon Hill once said, "Effort only fully releases its reward after a person refuses to quit." The biggest factor between those who pursue success to the end and those who do not is the willingness to fail. Most say they are willing to do what it takes, but few are willing to face the consequences that are associated with the journey.

Many years ago, two brothers from Elkhart, Kansas had a regular job at the local school. Their job was to start a fire in the classroom's potbellied stove every morning. One morning, one of the boys grabbed what he thought was a can of kerosene, poured it on the wood in the stove, and lit it. What he didn't know is that someone had replaced the kerosene with gasoline. The explosion killed the older brother, and severely damaged the younger brother's legs.

A doctor recommended amputating both legs. The parents refused, choosing instead to believe the legs would heal. When they removed the boy's bandages, they discovered that his right leg was three inches shorter than his left. The toes on the left leg had been almost burned off.

The courageous young boy did not let these "minor" injuries deter him. Despite the excruciating pain, he exercised daily so that he could walk again. Soon he took a few steps. Then came the walking. Before long he threw away the crutches. Still not satisfied, this undaunted young man began to run. Once he began to run, he never stopped.

This remarkable individual is Glen Cunningham. He was the first man to run a mile under three minutes. Once thought humanly impossible, he broke through that barrier. Cunningham, once known as "The World's Fastest Human Being," was named athlete of the century at Madison Square Garden.

Coming so close to loosing his legs, never walking again much less to run, he overcame great adversity. What was different about this man? He had determination and belief in himself. He knew he had the potential. Realizing this drove him through all the hardships. His refusal to give in paid off when he set the world record.

Realization. When awakening the potential within us, we have to realize who we really are. Only you know what you are capable of doing. We too often listen to what others think we can do. This limits us to their expectations. Sometimes a person can be encouraging, but they might have no idea how realistic their encouragement is.

Realization also means understanding that our potential is God-given. This humble realization keeps arrogance at bay. We must not think of ourselves too great for our accomplishments. Remember Theodore Roosevelt's statement, "Keep your eyes on the stars and your feet on the ground." This step alone will take you closer to real fulfillment and accomplishment than anything else.

Oliver Wendell Holmes said, "The biggest tragedy in America is not the great waste of natural resources, though this is tragic. The biggest tragedy is the waste of human resources." Mr. Holmes pointed out that the average person goes to his grave with his music still in him. The most beautiful melodies are usually the unplayed ones.

Many would consider it tragic for a dying man to discover a diamond mine in his backyard. This is no more tragic than anyone's life having un-mined and unnoticed potential. We have a great amount of wealth within us that if left untapped will lie there and never make a sound. It is up to us to release this vast amount of potential before we can sing our song in life.

What is your song? What music would you like to sing? Why are you not singing this tune? Natural resources will remain and can be used by future generations. Our "natural resources" only go to waste if we do not use them. The purpose of this book is to bring out these resources by first making you understand they are present and next creating a yearning desire for you to unleash them.

Only you can use the resources within. If you think little of yourself, if you consider yourself unworthy, this stops you from tapping into those resources. What you think about yourself is directly related to who you will become. What goes into your mind plays a major role in who you will become as well. Zig Ziglar said it best when he said, "You are what you are and where you are because of what goes into your mind. You can change what you are and where you are by changing what goes into your mind."

Think about that statement for a moment. Your mind plays *the* main role in determining where you will go in life. If you allow junk to go in, junk will come out. If you allow only positive to go, in then positive will come out. It's just that simple.

One of the saddest statements to hear from a person is "I wish I could." The fact of the matter is *you can!* You possess the ability to do what your heart's desire is and go where your heart leads you. Just like the oil well that is never discovered, you have the choice of never tapping into the endless amount of potential and energy that exist within you. The most difficult part of this process is the recognition of your abilities. Once you have done that, the rest should come natural. There are five steps to turning your potential into peak performance and making things happen in your life. I have listed them for you below.

Five Steps to Developing Your Potential

1. Self-image
In order to perform at your peak, it is imperative that you have a healthy self-image. The way you see yourself is, for all practical purposes, the way you will perform. As you release the real unlimited potential within yourself, the next step is putting it to use.

As I said earlier, you cannot perform in a manner inconsistent with the way you see yourself. Poor self-images may begin during childhood and continue throughout life. There are certain steps to improve how you see yourself. Look at these ways to develop a healthy self-image:

Recognize that you may not have one. If you do not see yourself in an overly positive way, you may need to develop a healthy self-image. If you don't believe you have the natural resources spoken of above, you need to change the way you see yourself. Realizing you need to beef up your self-image opens you up to the following steps.

God didn't make any losers. You were created in the image of God. To say you are ugly, you are a nobody, or you aren't good enough is a slap in the face of your Creator. No one is any better than you are. Although your talents may be different than others, they are no better or worse than the person next to you in His eyes. Start your day by looking in the mirror and saying "God loves me, and I am somebody." If someone has told you that you are not, they are the ones with the problems.

Listen to the positive. Let speakers, teachers and preachers that teach the clean, the pure and the positive infuse you. Listen to motivational and inspirational tapes that build you up and let you know that you are a unique individual unlike anyone else.

Learn to smile and greet people with enthusiasm. Regardless of how your day is going smile and project happiness. It is an unavoidable truth. If you set your attitude, you'll affect your altitude. Try it. You will be happier and feel better about yourself.

Be cautious with whom you associate with. If you associate with winners, you will start thinking like a winner. If you associate with losers that pull everyone down around them, you will begin thinking like them as well. I coined the phrase "outhouse syndrome." Hanging out in an outhouse long enough may not make you one, but you will start smelling like one. Choose your friends carefully.

Learn to speak in public. Join a group such as Toast Masters International or CLASS. These types of groups are not formed to embarrass you but rather to build you up. They are made up of people just like you. The greatest fear among people today is speaking in public. To some it's more frightening than dying itself. Anyone who speaks will tell you, however, that there is no better way to build self-image than to speak in front of a group of people.

Look people in the eye. Nothing impacts like eye contact while speaking. Eye to eye contact builds self-esteem and creates a sense of worthiness. Eye contact reveals truth, character and integrity.

Avoid those things that degrade. Pornography and graphic violence cheapens life. Violence depicts life as nothing more than a vapor without value. Pornography cheapens women, negatively impacting marital intimacy. The eyes are the windows of the soul. Explicit material burns its negativity into the mind. Do not let anything negative in your mind. It will eventually tear down your self-image.

Watch you appearance. Your physical body is the first thing others see of you. It is what you see every time you look in the mirror. Pay attention to your dress. Develop a comfortable but appropriate style. Changing your appearance can dramatically change your self-image. Loosing a few pounds, buying some new but affordable clothes, even changing your hairstyle can make you feel like a new person. When it is possible alter your appearance. The bottom line is, take care of yourself. The positive impact will amaze you.

2. Take aim
This is the second step in developing your potential. Many people follow the method: ready, fire, aim. Unless you are Butch Cassidy or the Sundance Kid, you are unlikely to hit anything. You will seldom arrive at a destination that you haven't planned for. As a child my friend loathed getting in the car driving around town trying to decide where his family would eat supper. To this day he will not get in the car until they first decide where they're eating. Decide what you want in life and take aim.

3. Passionately pursue what you want.
There is much talk about setting goals. But unless you aggressively go after what you desire, what's the use? Passionately go after what

you set your sites on. Be willing to sacrifice for it. What is the benefit of aiming at something if you don't shoot?

4. Take action by abolishing procrastination from your life
Procrastination is the thief of your life's dreams. As I stated before, most people have multiple *wants* for every *do* in their life. Regardless of what you desire to accomplish there is no time like the present. You must want before you can do and *you must do before you can have.* If you have been wrestling with a particular desire for your life, begin now doing something about it. Perhaps the greatest gap in life is the one between knowing and doing. It's the procrastination gap. Procrastination is the subtle art of sabotaging your potential. The procrastinator spends a lifetime in the twilight zone between thinking and doing. The result is over-analyzing and underachieving. Learn to act and be decisive, eliminating procrastination from your life.

5. Be flexible
As you pursue your dreams, there will be times that the goals you have established for yourself or the way you are approaching them will require change. It is only natural. Your dreams will change; your tastes will mature. Throughout life use these little adjustments in your vision to zero in on your target. Don't become inflexible. We all have a natural resistance to change. Even when chasing your dreams you can find yourself in a rut. Situations may change. As they do be open to fine tune your vision and redefine your dreams.

You can develop your potential and be a peak performer because you have what it takes. You just have to tap into the potential we are talking about. Although there are risks involved when we strive for anything beyond our comfort zone you must learn to turn risk into results. Face your fears. Do not be afraid to "go where no man has gone before." Possess imagination, spirit, courage, convictions, responsibility, character, integrity and a perception that stimulates change.

Being a peak performer is not something that everyone is cut out to be. Yet the potential to be just that lies within each and every one of us. The next time you see someone doing something that you think you are capable of doing, you probably are! The problem with most people is not in the developing of their potential but rather in finding it in the first place. If I can see, smell, taste, touch and hear something, I believe it exists. Take away those physical senses, however, and it's a whole different ballgame. This is the concept I want you to take away from reading this book. You have to change yourself to be all you can be. You have what it takes to be all that you were designed to be.

The Parable of the Talents

Most of you remember the story in the Bible concerning the talents. One man was given one, the other two, and the last one had five. The Lord went away for a long time. When He returned, He asked the one with five talents what he had done. The man replied he had put them to work and he now had ten. The Lord replied to him, "Well done my good and faithful servant, because you have been good in using what I have given you I will give you more." The one who had two talents had also multiplied his two into four and the Lord replied the same way. Then came the last one that was given only one talent. He was asked as the others. He replied that he buried his and still had only the one talent. To that the Lord replied, "Thou wicked and slothful servant." He then took his talent and gave it to the one with many.

So what is the moral of this story, and how does it relate to what we are talking about? **Take what you have, and use it and you will receive more rewards!** To those that complain about the rich getting richer and the poor getting poorer the Bible says, "To him that has, more shall be given." Remember, the value of money is no more than the jar it's in if no one discovers it. Your true value or potential is also of little value until you discover and release it.

Yearn to release your unlimited potential. Realize that the limitations you may establish on yourself come from within the confines of your own mind. The five-minute mile was, for a long time, the ultimate record for the speed runner. Once it was broken it seemed everyone who attempted was holding back because many followed. The same goes for many other feats among the population. If something is accomplished and proven to be safe then many will follow. It takes a peak performer to make it happen alone. That desire to step out of your comfort zone is the yearning that I'm speaking of.

Are you satisfied with what you are doing with your life? If you could change something, would you? If so, what? My hope for you is that you desire to bring out your capabilities and develop them just as a body builder discovers his potential and develops his muscles. As with all things that have lasting meaning and effects, discovering it is the first and most difficult task.

CHANGE yOUrSELF

83

STRATEGY 8 : OVERCOME OBSTACLES

Long ago there was a king that had a boulder placed on a roadway. Then he hid himself and watched to see if anyone would remove the huge rock. Some of the king's wealthiest merchants and courtiers came by and simply walked around it. Many loudly blamed the king for not keeping the roads clear, but none did anything about getting the big stone out of the way. Then a peasant came along carrying a load of vegetables. On approaching the boulder, the peasant laid down his burden and tried to move the stone to the side of the road. After much pushing and straining, he finally succeeded. As the peasant picked up his load of vegetables, he noticed a purse lying in the road where the boulder had been. The purse contained many gold coins and a note from the king indicating that the gold was for the person who removed the boulder from the roadway. The peasant learned what others seldom understand. Every obstacle presents an opportunity to improve one's condition.

Life is full of *obstacle illusions*. They appear to block our path, but only exist in our minds. These illusions keep the majority of people from reaching their goals. Most of what we see as impossible feats in our life are just that, illusions. We do not try because we believe we can't. That belief comes from inside our minds and hearts and usually stems from what someone else told us we could or could not do.

Overcoming obstacles requires perseverance. Perseverance, the ability to " hang on" just a bit longer, is the single greatest determinant of your success.

There is a story about a boy born with clubfeet named Joey. The doctors assured his parents that with treatment he would be able to walk normally. But they cautioned that he would never be able to run. The first three years of his life were spent in surgery, casts and braces. By the time he was eight, you wouldn't know he had a problem by seeing him. The children in the neighborhood ran around as most children do during play, and Joey would jump right in and run and play too. His parents never told him that he wouldn't be able to run as well as the other children, so he never knew any different.

In the seventh grade he decided to try out for the cross-country team. Every day he trained with the team. He worked harder and ran more than any of the others. Perhaps he sensed that the abilities that seemed to come naturally to so many others did not come naturally to him. Although the entire team runs, only the fastest runners actually compete in the race. His parents never told him he probably would never make the team, so he didn't know.

Joey continued to run four to five miles a day, every day even the day he had a 103-degree fever. His family was worried, so they went to look for him after school. They found him running all alone. When they asked him how he felt, he said, "Okay," and continued to run two more miles. The sweat ran down his face and his eyes were glassy from his fever. Yet he looked straight ahead and kept running. He was never told he couldn't run with a 103-degree fever, so he didn't know.

Two weeks later, the names of the team runners were called. Joey was number six on the list. He had made the team. Joey was in the seventh grade—the other team members were all eighth graders. He was never told he shouldn't expect to make the team. He was never told he couldn't do it. His parents never told him he couldn't do it, so he didn't know. He just did it.

There is a lot to be learned from that story. Obstacles arise in all shapes and sizes. As I said at the beginning of this strategy however, most obstacles are illusions. They seem like mountains that are insurmountable, yet when faced, most change from large to small. We pass right over them as if they never existed.

Throughout this strategy we are going to look squarely in the eyes of failure. Anyone that has accomplished anything of significance has faced obstacles in their lifetime. Most would tell you that at the time of confrontation it seemed like defeat was inevitable. Charles A. Lindbergh once said, "Success is not measured by what a man accomplishes, but by the opposition he has encountered, and the courage with which he has maintained the struggle against overwhelming odds." Truer words have not been spoken. It is the ability to overcome that separates the winners from the losers, mediocrity from peak performance.

A boy named Sparky had his share of obstacles in life. For Sparky, school was all but impossible. He failed every subject in the eight grade. He flunked physics in high school, getting a grade of zero. Sparky also flunked Latin, algebra and English. He didn't do much better in sports. Although he did manage to make the school's golf team, he lost the only important match of the season.

Throughout his youth Sparky was awkward socially. No one seemed to care much for him. Just hearing a classmate saying hello would astonish him. In high school, he never asked a girl for a date. Sparky was too afraid of being turned down. He was a loser and everyone knew it. *He* made up his mind early in life that if things were meant to work out, they would.

But there was one thing important to Sparky. He loved to draw. He was proud of his artwork. Of course, no one else appreciated it. In his senior year of high school he submitted some cartoons to the editors of the yearbook. They were turned down. Despite this particular rejection, Sparky was so convinced of his ability that he decided to become a professional artist. After completing high school, he wrote a letter to Walt Disney Studios. He was told to send some more samples of his work, and the subject for a cartoon was suggested. Sparky drew the proposed cartoon and submitted it. Finally the reply came from them. He had been rejected once again.

Ultimately Sparky decided to tell about his own life in a cartoon. The main character, a loser who had never met the expectations of others, described his childhood. The cartoon soon became famous worldwide. The boy named Sparky we know as Charles Schulz. The cartoon many have grown up with is "Peanuts." And of course, the little cartoon character that never succeeded was Charlie Brown.

What would have happened if Mr. Schulz had given up? Do you believe that because of his talent people would have knocked on his door? That's doubtful. He had to pursue his dream until someone would listen. Although in many areas of his life he could be considered a loser, he knew he was a winner at drawing. That was his talent. That was his vision. That became his destiny in life.

Others have pursued their dreams against overwhelming odds as well. As a matter of fact, most that now bask in the sun of success and pleasure have once cooked on the stove of pain. The pain, the by-product of learning the ropes of life, laid the foundation for future success. Without it our dreams would topple. We are all familiar with the tragic stories of individuals to whom success and fame came too early. Child stars that couldn't handle the wealth at such a young age crumbled under the pressure.

Many have built their success on foundations of failure. Walt Disney was said to have gone bankrupt five times before maintaining success. Alex Haley was rejected 300 times for his manuscript of *Roots*. Fred Ester was told he couldn't dance. He was bald headed, and he couldn't sing either! Abraham Lincoln failed most of his political career before eventually becoming President of the United States. Colonel Sanders was rejected 1,000 times before he received his first *yes* concerning his fried chicken recipe. Steven Spielberg confronted every possible obstacle before becoming the most successful producer in Hollywood.

Thomas Edison had 10,000 failures before finding a way to make the light bulb work. When asked he said that he only found 10,000 ways it would not work. He continued to work until he had found the secret to the incandescent light bulb. Just think if he had listened to the negative voices so common in the world in which we live.

I could go on and on with success story after success story, but hopefully you are getting the picture. The path of least resistance is what makes rivers and men crooked. The path of hardest resistance is what makes rivers and men straight. Those things that persist always thrive. Those things that only try never remain alive. The average businessman often doesn't understand that success is a contrast to its failures. Walking is but a process of falling forward. You fall, catch yourself, step forward to save yourself and then fall again. Thus you move forward.

Where are you in life, and where are you going? Are you fearful of what may happen if you attempt and fail? For all that strive forward, faith must be the underlying factor. *Fear sees the obstacle, while faith sees the opportunity.* Our attitude limits our behavior. These limitations cause us to miss out on the magnificent gifts that life has to offer.

The analogy of flea training tells this story well. If you place fleas in a jar with the lid on they will attempt to jump out of the jar. Their efforts prove unsuccessful because the lid limits their attempts for freedom. A funny thing happens after a while. The fleas become conditioned to their circumstances. Removing the lid does not allow them to escape. They never again try to jump higher than their past failures. Although freedom is just a fraction of an inch away, it may as well be a mile.

This type of mental limitation causes us to miss achieving peak performance. Things do not get done because we have been told they can't. These obstacle illusions are just opportunities in disguise, opportunities to grow from triumphing over the seemingly insurmountable mountains, through positive action. Positive action enables us to persevere. Perseverance is the key to climbing the mountain to success, done through positive action, not negative acceptance. Ask yourself this question: Am I positive or negative in my attitude? I can assure you that if you wish to be a peak performer, seeing things with positive eyes will bring you much closer to that goal. How do you know if you are a positive person? Let's take a look at some facts about positive people.

Facts About Positive People
- They are excited about life
- They are filled with enthusiasm
- They look ahead not behind
- They are creative
- They are likeable (once you get to know them)
- They are friendly
- They look for good in bad situations
- They are progressive in their thinking
- They are motivated by dreams and have definite goals

- They are success oriented and visualize themselves as a success
- They constantly stretch their minds so they won't ever think small

Reflecting on the names of those we discussed earlier, how many of them do you think had negative attitudes? We have heard a lot about positive attitudes and their effect on our outcome, but how many of us really take it to heart? You may say that I don't know your circumstances. That's true. The fact of the matter is that you don't know mine either.

There was a time when I was confronted with a crisis. I didn't think there was any way out. Faced with seemingly insurmountable debt and in a destructive partnership, I realized I had two choices. The first was to allow that crisis to ruin me. The second choice was to learn from my mistakes and attempt to turn the crisis into an opportunity for my wife and me.

I chose the latter. I was told I couldn't change the inevitable and that I was destined for bankruptcy. My life felt like it was falling apart. I began to learn all I could about money, leadership and most importantly how to be the best husband and father I could be.

What I learned was simple yet life changing. Regardless of what situation you are in, there is a way to make positive out of the negative. With time and the grace of God I overcame those obstacles as so many others have that made up their minds to do it.

Adam Walsh transformed a tragedy into an opportunity to help others in similar situations. His son was kidnapped. After searching some time for him, Adam's son was found—dead. No one knew who had committed this horrible act.

For most that would be enough to cause you to leave this world yourself. But not Adam. He chose a positive path. Fighting for the creation of a national TV show, "America's Most Wanted." Each week he tried to keep other people from going through the tragedy he endured. It didn't bring his son back, but it did make a difference.

I understand all too well that there are times when it seems impossible to keep your head high, when life feels like it has a hold on you rather than you having a hold on it. But it's your choice. You can choose to be the rider or the ridden. You can turn the negative circumstances into positive.

The reasons to be positive are many, but for the sake of being concise I have made a list below of the reasons you and I should be positive.

Reasons To Be Positive

You have everything of which to be glad and nothing of which to be sad. Life may deal you a bad hand, but you still have a chance because you still have hope. God Himself has a plan for you. Place your hope in that He is working the plan out. Choose to encourage yourself with this.

There is nothing you can't accomplish with the help of your creator. The Bible says that God has "called us out of darkness into His marvelous light." Speaking of those He has called, "Faithful is He who calls you, and He also will bring it to pass." "'For I know the plans that I have for you,' declares the LORD, 'plans for welfare and not for calamity to give you a future and a hope.'"

If you have nothing else, you have this day, so make the best of it. At the time of this writing, my wife suffered the loss of her brother. Things such as this cause us to realize the brevity of life and the desire to breathe in every oxygen molecule we can. Don't let a moment go by that you don't tell someone you love him or her. There is no guarantee that you will ever see them again.

In every failure is the seed of success. *Failure is an event not a destination.* As I have said so many times before, failure breeds success. It simply teaches you ways that do not work, which brings you closer to your ultimate goal.

You were born to win. Each one of us was born to win in life. God didn't create losers. You were created to win at the game of life. Begin reaching down inside of yourself to discover what you are made out of. There is no mountain too large, no obstacle so big that you can't overcome it. How often do we hear people say they "can't" do something? You can because you were created to win not to loose. Winning may not be everything in life but the *effort to win* is.

As you encounter life's obstacles understand that small things make winners. First, focus your time and energy on the achievement of your dreams. By doing so you can see right through the mountains that stand in your way. In the martial arts you are taught to look through the target in which you are striking. The reason for this is to focus your energy. In our seminars we have had people attempt to overcome certain obstacles that they thought were otherwise impossible. I have seen 70-year-old men and petite women break boards with the palm of their hands as if they were toothpicks. They just believed. It's only when we place the limitations in our own minds that we remain where we are in life.

A perfect example of this is how elephants respond to what they think are their limitations. When training an elephant to stay in a specific area, a chain is placed on the elephant's leg. After a period of time the chain can be removed and the elephant will walk in the same circle as if still bound by the chain.

How many of us have chains on our legs preventing us from moving forward? Isn't it time you removed them?

The next small thing that makes winners is avoiding toxic people. You should hang out with people that have done what you want to do. Instead many are influenced by people that drain the positive out of them. Being told you can't do something creates the image of obstacles being impassable. The bottom line is watch who you associate with on a regular basis.

Last, take full responsibility for your mistakes. Remember this simple formula when thinking of how we respond to events in our life: **E + R =O**. The E stands for events. These are the things that come our way and cause us to respond or react. The R stands for response. If we respond to our events, odds are that we can successfully overcome them. If, on the other hand, we react to them, the chances are they will prevail. The O stands for outcome. It goes without saying that our outcome is determined by the way we respond to our events in life, particularly obstacles that come our way.

It's the small things in life that create the positive mindset we so desperately need. A small thing once killed a giant. When David saw Goliath, he didn't see what everyone else saw. He saw someone that was in the way and needed to be removed! We all have giants that need to be removed in our life. The only way to remove them is to face them head on.

Giants then have a funny way of getting smaller and smaller. These giants that we are referring to as obstacles, will devour the very spirit of your being if you allow them to. Approach them with caution and wisdom, but by all means don't avoid them. That will only make them appear larger. Maintain the attitude that you can do all things through your creator. Your attitude is the very essence of your success. *When you find out a man's thoughts, you find the true measure of a man.* If you want to find out how one thinks just hang around them for a while. The mouth has a way of telling the true story of our heart.

Our attitude determines much of the way we view ourselves. We must run from arrogance but strive for self-confidence. The difference between the two is like night and day. Arrogant people believe the world revolves around them while self-confident people believe they can make a difference in the world. We make a difference when we use our weaknesses to the benefit of others and ourselves.

When faced with obstacles our world seems to cave in. If we realize that they are merely learning experiences, we can make opportunities out of them. If we look at them the way the world does, we will react the way the world does by caving in to fear and failure. The only way to overcome these destructive forces is to face them, as we should giants and view them as opportunities. Very seldom will you find a giant that doesn't produce an opportunity once confronted and overcome. Realize you are in a battle, a war for right and wrong, good and bad, success and failure. The battle never ends, but you can learn the rules to the fight. By knowing the rules and having somewhat of an understanding of what is on the other side, the war doesn't seem as large as it once did.

CHANGE yoUrself

95

STRATEGY 9 : UNDERSTAND THE DIFFERENCE : BETWEEN LIVING : AND EXISTING

We have discussed in previous strategies that what dominates our minds may very well determine where we go in life. Understanding that fact, it is important that we be aware of all life has to offer. If we are going to become peak performers, it stands to reason that living life to its fullest is something we must not take for granted.

Many people are smiling, happy and appear full of joy but without anyone knowing they are dying on the inside. Anyone ever losing someone close to them has walked this road. The purpose of this book is to get you to act and take the necessary steps to becoming a peak performer. On the other hand the last thing I want you to do is to go through life striving to be all you can and never *living as who you are*. It is extremely important that we strive for progress without loosing our identity.

When I first started on the speaking circuit I struggled somewhat. It sometimes seemed I was more concerned with saying what I thought people would like to hear. I quickly realized that what I was feeling led to say was usually what people needed to hear the most. As a progress maker we simply must make progress our only viable option. If we choose any other, we are choosing to be a progress taker.

To recap on some things we covered in strategy one, progress makers do the following:

1. Stop thinking tomorrow is going to be different unless you make it so.
2. Develop a plan of action to lead you to your ultimate outcome and be willing to change if necessary.
3. Follow a plan through by making it an absolute necessity.

To be a peak performer, your interest should lie in creating a life, not just living one. What does this phrase actually mean? The answer lies in understanding the difference between living and just existing. To live means to create: to exist means to stagnate. If you are living, you are continuously planning without becoming complacent. True living does, however, breed contentment. To be satisfied with who you are is good. To become lazy is not. To perform at our peak it is imperative that we embrace the philosophy of change that we have spoken of so intensely in previous strategies.

Most who only exist have no understanding of the word change. They listen and want but continue to do the same things. When we analyze the difference between two totally opposite people we must ask ourselves what exactly makes them different? I'm not talking about fame or fortune but rather the very spirit of the person.

Take two very well known but distinctly different people such as Jim Jones and Billy Graham. Both have or had a mission and vision for their lives and the lives of those they came in contact with. Yet one was a legendary killer leading people in the wrong direction, and the other led people to a loving knowledge of God. What was the difference between these two men? Simply speaking, it was what went into their minds, or should I say, what they allowed to go into their minds.

The mind has a direct access to the heart. If we are to excel, we need to guard it with all our might. We are, in essence, what we allow ourselves to think. The old saying, "We are what we are and where we are because of what goes into our minds" is nothing less than the truth. What you allow to dominate your mind influences your life. It literally will determine who and what you will become. *You will never rise above the level of your lowest thoughts, and likewise, you will never fall beneath the level of your lowest thoughts.* Truer words have never been spoken.

To live means to be happy and fulfilled in all aspects of your life. Even in the bad times a person that truly understands the meaning of living focuses on the good surrounding them. All of us have faced bad times at one time or another. Many who only exist may find themselves in a "funnel" feeling like there is no way out. To truly live life to its fullest involves looking past adversity, seeing the hope not despair. Depression strikes when the choice is made not to hope. They believe there is no possibility for a good outcome. Loosing the zest for life, they can even loose the will to live.

There is quite a difference between living and merely existing. A rock exists, but it does not live. Many people, whom we assume are alive, really only sit around like a rock. They just exist, no expectations. Others cling to the side of a rock, fearing they will plummet into the chasm. They exist in continuous fear.

Do you live, or do you merely exist? Here are ten things that can help you decide for yourself. Do you—

1. Look at life as a blessing from God, giving thanks everyday
for the chance to make a difference
2. Be content with who and what you are, always striving to become better in all areas of life
3. Desire to win at the game of life
4. Realize that the only thing in life that shouldn't change is priorities (if they are in the right order)
5. Forgive others and forget the past
6. Balance your lives between work and play
7. Stick to the truth no matter what
8. Realize the difference between friends and acquaintances
and cherish both in their own ways
9. Face your fears head on
10. Live life to its fullest, realizing there is nothing more precious

As you can see, living is much more than breathing, walking and talking. Are you living life to it's fullest? Is what people see on the outside of you the same that's on the inside? Put another way, are you the same person when no one is looking? If not, maybe it's time you re-evaluated your life to find out what is keeping you from being all you are capable of being. Controlling our thought life has a significant impact on what we are, and who we will become.

Think about the times you have been at your best. Things seemed to be going your way. When these times come along in our lives, we feel a sense of what living is all about. Examining these times further you will find that your thought life was in a state of positive consciousness. For example if you are in a conflict with someone you love, your whole life is affected. You may be able to hide it on the outside; however, beneath the outer shell you are not all you can be. Your thought process is affected. Anyone will tell you that they perform better when their personal life is in order.

This illustrates how thoughts have a direct impact on our hearts as they guide us through life. It is by our hearts that we say the things we say, do the things we do and eventually become what we become. So many people waste their lives always letting things slip to tomorrow. If something is not done today, that's okay because there will be another time. This type of thinking is what ultimately causes so many regrets. If we are going to be top performers we have to start looking at today as the *only* day we have.

Two individuals come to mind that have made such a significant impact on this earth. The first is a man that once was a radio announcer in Davenport, Iowa. Later he became a movie star, going on to become the President of the United States. You probably know whom I'm talking about. His name is Ronald Reagan. It's obvious that he has lived his life to its fullest, taking advantage of every moment he was given.

Another example, which I've mentioned earlier, is Billy Graham. Here is a man that dedicated his life to winning souls for the cause of Christ. Wherever he goes he can fill a stadium. Everybody respects him. Has he made an impact? You bet!

Have both of these men realized that living is different than existing? I believe so. Both were married, both had children that they loved dearly. Both saw past what life had to offer them. They took the initiative. Not once, but at every opportunity. They excelled and will someday be written about in history books.

Using these two great men as examples does not mean that you have to make an impact on the world to really live life to its fullest. You can excel in life no matter who you are. Guarding your mind against thoughts that would limit you while protecting your heart against attitudes that would rob you of hope, allows you to live that life. Choosing to view life from a positive perspective enables you to see over the horizon of what life has to offer. It transforms the negative situations handed you into positive actions you can take.

This is why having a positive attitude is so important. A negative viewpoint fogs your vision. You cannot see the opportunities up ahead. You lose hope, sink even lower and eventually give up. It is crucial that you learn to turn the negative into the positive.

Keys to Create Positive Thinking in Your Life

Make it a habit to focus on what you do have rather than what you don't have. Make positive thinking a habit rather than something you have to think about doing. We live in a negative world where good news is no news. Concentrate on those things that cause you to see the best in every situation.

Take the *seven-day test*. For seven consecutive days attempt to think of nothing but positive thoughts. If you mess up and think of something negative you have to start over. You will confront something negative within that period of time, and learning to overcome it will be your first step to becoming the peak performer that lives life to it's fullest.

If you will do this exercise for seven consecutive days, it will make a difference in your life. It will be noticeable to you and to those around you.

Decide right now to become curious rather than being judgmental. Have the desire to find out what is really going on. Learn to perceive more and judge less. Things aren't always as they appear to be. The very people you believe are jerks, mean or stuck up may merely be victims themselves. They can go to great lengths to protect themselves, and you don't know it. Be curious rather than rush to judgment. Remember what Jesus said, "He who is without sin cast the first stone."

Practice seeing the positive side of anything negative. Make a conscious effort to find the positive. Most situations have positive aspects if you can find them. You might only be able to say that it could have been much worse, but by exercising your positive perspective you substantially improve your attitude.

Realize you are not going to be perfect. Trying to be the best you can be is something we all should strive for. However, we must realize that we will never be perfect. Being a perfectionist only sets us up for pain and failure. We will make mistakes. Our goal should be to get a little better with each passing day, not perfect.

Develop faith in your life in the face of your circumstances. With everything you confront, face it with certainty. Have the courage to overcome your fears and face whatever comes your way. Live with a trust in the Creator. You can never cover all the bases. You do your best and then trust.

If asked, could you list all the important events that happened to you the past five years? Some people cannot. Some cannot remember any details. No fun moments. No memories. Just life without living.

You may ask what significance this has on being a peak performer. Life so easily passes us by. Whether you're always on the go or on the couch, life without meaning is life wasted. In five years what will you remember?

The magic question is how do I know I'm living and not just existing. The answer comes in one word: *Fruit.* The fruit you bear in your life will tell what your life has stood for. This is the key in living. An apple tree is a living thing—it produces fruit. A rock cannot do that. It cannot produce anything nor add to itself. We know we are alive when we produce fruit, something that nourishes. Fruit benefits others. In the same way we know that we are more than existing when we help others.

We can look after ourselves, but this is not living. Being busy is not living either. A dead leaf can spin in the wind. It is not alive though. We can strive for our own success. Striving to get to the top of the corporate ladder. Striving to make more money. Striving, striving, striving and forgetting those that we love. Trust me when I tell you that no one achieves success that loses or neglects those that he loves.

I do want to clarify something though. There are some people that remain alone during their life and are fulfilled. They do, however, find joy in helping others, sharing their love and the love of their creator with those they come in contact with.

The fruit we bear is in essence what we have to show for our efforts, not just materialistically but also spiritually. I remember the old Frankenstein movies. Dr. Frankenstein would dig up a corpse and bring it back to life. I used to set on the edge of my seat waiting for the monster to come alive! Then came the words, *"It's alive, it's alive!* Man that would really scare me.

He was alive, but he never really *lived.* So many people today are like Frankenstein. They are alive, but they never really live. They desire to, just as the monster did, but their life seems to have no meaning for them. They search for the answers, but few find them. They go from day to day and couldn't tell you what happened yesterday nor do they care. Their life is full of being full, but monotony is at the core of everything they do. What are we working so hard for if we never take a moment to smell the roses?

No matter how great our vision is, we have to take time for ourselves and those we love. Being Frankenstein is not any way to live your life. You may never write a book, be on television, speak to a thousand people or touch the lives of the masses. That's perfectly all right. What matters is that you do what *you* were meant to do.

Each of us has a destiny. If we considered how fragile life is, the world would be a different place. Have you ever noticed how people act when they loose a loved one or attend a funeral? Suddenly life takes on a new meaning. I have often witnessed people make promises about their life after the death of someone close to them. But little by little they seem to forget what that moment brought to them.

If you fall into this category of existing and not living, I urge you to take a close look at your life. There are no guarantees of tomorrow, but you do have an opportunity today. The opportunity exists to prioritize your life and become the person you were created to be.

You have what it takes to reach the highest mountain and swim the widest sea because you have God Himself on your side. Don't let any one tell you again that you can't do something because you are not good enough. By living today, you can reap life's crop tomorrow. You can make things happen in your life. It's strictly up to you. Choose to live rather than exist. By doing so you will not only accomplish more, you will be living to enjoy it.

Below is a poem concerning this very subject. It has been repeated to me several times during my life. I believe it sums up this strategy and drives the point home directly into our hearts where it belongs.

Living And Dying

There was a very cautious man,
He rarely laughed,
He rarely cried,
He rarely risked,
He rarely tried,
He rarely sang,
He rarely played,
He rarely laughed,
He rarely prayed,
And then one day he passed away but his
      insurance policy wouldn't pay,
They said he lied,
Because he never really lived,
Therefore he never really died.

—Author Unknown

CHANGE youRSELF

105

STRATEGY 10 : REACH FOR THE STARS

The first nine strategies have concentrated on the foundation of becoming a peak performer and making things happen in your life. Now we will begin our journey into building on that foundation. Now is the time to reach for the stars.

All of us desire to achieve some type of success during our lifetimes. The very fact that you are reading this book indicates that you are interested in creating a life not just having one. The problem for many attempting to climb the success ladder often revolves around how. Although we have discussed many of the components necessary to answer this question, there are still several to explore.

It is my firm belief that, if you follow the same principles and concepts practiced by those that have achieved success in their life, you can achieve the same in yours. If we do not do what we know we should do, we are taking *possibility* out of the equation. We may be capable, but the possibility is slim to none that we will accomplish what we desire.

There are no shortages of success formulas. In fact, there are probably more available than you care to read. All, however, have one thing in common. They all attempt to get us to make a change.

Here I will concentrate on the master keys to creating success and achievement. The first one we studied in depth in strategy one. We can then be brief in its explanation.

Have A Willingness to Learn and Change as Necessary

This is one of the most crucial steps in becoming successful in business and life. So important that I feel it deserves a second look.

Some people with unsuccessful businesses baffle me. Closing their minds to any help, they appear to want to fail. They ask questions but do not listen to the answers. Blindly they are convinced their path is the right one. Despite indications otherwise, they cannot be persuaded there is a better way.

Often the belief in their inevitable success is not based on the plan's merit. Certain laziness can keep us from considering change. Change can be the hardest part of life. We condition ourselves to avoid it. But without it we are doomed to failure.

Learning new things and adapting the principles to our game plan helps us avoid tunnel vision. It is essential that we continue to grow and adapt as we go along. Accept that you can always learn. Strive for the knowledge to improve. This is the first step towards achieving the success you desire.

Decide What You *Really* Want and Break Out of Your Comfort Zone

Many talk about what they want in life, but few are willing to make the sacrifices to attain it. Wanting something is meaningless without action. Action only comes by having a burning desire. That passion must be present in every peak performer's life.

Passion begins with knowing what you want. Focusing on that desire builds a fire in us. We become motivated and single-minded. Not knowing what we really want snuffs out the flame within. Not able to focus, our desire tumbles from one thing to the next like a leaf blowing in the wind.

Not having any passion, we are not motivated to break out of our comfort zone. That zone bogs us down. We don't want to stretch or take chances—all things we must do to be successful. Some are motivated by money, but it seldom brings happiness. Although money is necessary, it is merely a yardstick of the service we render. When it becomes the object of our desire, it becomes hollow.

Passion, then, becomes important in achieving success. It gets us out of our comfort zones, and it allows us to focus on what we truly desire. Build passion in your life by determining what you want to accomplish. Focus on what is important. Then let it motivate you.

Write Down Your Goals

As mentioned in a previous strategy, you seldom hit what you don't aim at. That's the whole basis of reaching for the stars. When you determine your passion in life, aim at it. Take advantage of the motivation passion brings. Write down you passions. They then become goals.

The difference between a train and a ship helps illustrate the need for written goals. A train has its course laid out for it. It can only follow the tracks. If an obstruction blocks its way, the train must wait for it to be cleared. A train's future potential depends on whomever laid out its course.

A ship, however, is free to chart its own course. If a storm looms up ahead, the ship can change its heading. The pilot only need point the bow.

Many people feel stuck on the tracks of another's laying. They don't feel life is going in the right direction. They presume that they can only proceed forward along imagined tracks. Setting goals lets you jump the tracks. Writing them down lets you chart your own course.

The thought of writing down your goals scares some and makes other people wary. The term *goals* has become a buzzword having lost its meaning. People have been burned by unrealistic expectations. Despite this, using goals is necessary to take control of your course. Let me assure you that if you are going to attain peak performance, goal setting will need to be a significant part of your life.

Guidelines for Goal Setting

Be honest with yourself. If you are headed west, believing you are heading south will not change your direction. It will cause you to be more determined, blinded and defiant to the truth. You will head further toward the wrong destination. Be completely honest about where you're heading in life and whether you are willing to change directions.

It seems no matter what we discuss, the word change comes into play. Hopefully by now you realize the importance of change. Be sure the goals you establish are made for you. Many try to establish goals such as wanting to be or look like another. These types of goals only lead to disappointment. They have no place in a peak performer's life. You are an individual with your own qualities, and you need to sing your own song. Be who God made you to be.

There is a story of a scorpion and a frog that illustrates the role our identity plays in determining our actions. The scorpion wanted to get to the other side of a pond and asked the frog for a ride on his back. The frog said, "No. Because you are a scorpion, you will sting me causing me to drown." The scorpion laughed and told the frog how stupid that assumption was because he would drown also if he stung him. To that the frog conceded and allowed the scorpion on his back. Half way across the pond the scorpion stung the frog. The frog was devastated and told the scorpion that now they would both drown. When he asked why he stung him the scorpion replied, "I'm a scorpion. That's what I do."

The scorpion had a firm grasp of his purpose in life. He didn't pretend to be a bird, a fish, or a frog. We need to be realistic with expectations. A six foot eight, four-hundred-pound man will never be a jockey in the Kentucky Derby. Most of us will not be super models or become president of the United States. So be honest with yourself while setting goals. Be realistic too.

Be specific. When deciding where you want to be in life, a vague description will not get you there. You must be specific in your goal setting. "I want to retire in five years" is not a specific goal. It will not bring you closer to the goal than would staying home doing nothing.

Being specific in your goal setting will not only allow you to establish goals that are realistically attainable, but also place you on the path you have chosen for your life. If you have had difficulty in accomplishing your goals, I urge you to evaluate how specific they are. Until you know specifically what you want, you cannot lay out a plan to attain it, and with no plan there is no hope. Your goal will remain a dream, indefinitely.

Establish short and long term goals. As you reach for the stars, it is imperative that you do so both short and long term. A long-term goal without a short-term goal is like trying to run before learning to walk.

The short-term goals are the stepping-stones. Long-term goals are necessary to plan where we are going tomorrow. By looking far enough ahead, you can lay out a plan including the obstacles that you may confront along the way. Without long-term goals your future is left to chance. The short-term goals enable you to attain your long-term goals one step at a time.

Stay focused. It is difficult reaching a destination by looking back where you came from. Remain focused on the target ahead, resisting lesser concerns that bring distractions.

Much time was spent in strategy five on the topic of focus. It would be a good idea to go back and reread it. Focus is key to achieving success. It would be a discipline worthy of mastering. We are constantly bombarded with information geared at wooing us to fulfill another's goals. Like thieves, these people steal our focus and any hope of fulfilling our own goals.

Exercise your focus muscle every day. Review your goals daily. Choose daily which is more important, achieving your goals or chasing another rabbit.

Important questions. Three questions will assist you in preventing mistakes in goal setting. These questions evaluate your priorities in life. Setting goals without the right priorities guarantees your success leaving you unfulfilled. Answer these questions and you'll be on your way to setting fulfilling goals.

- Does this goal inflict pain on anyone?
- Will my goals cause me to turn my back on my creator and my loved ones, placing my priorities above their good?
- Does meditating and praying about my goals cause an "uneasiness" within my spirit?

Abolishing Procrastination in Your Life

As I have stated before, procrastination is the thief of your life's dreams. Regardless of your life's desires, there is no time like the present. Reaching for the stars is common for the peak performer.

Perhaps the greatest gap in life is the one between knowing and doing. It's the procrastination gap. Procrastination is the subtle art of sabotaging your potential. The procrastinator spends a lifetime in the twilight zone between thinking and doing. The result is over-analyzing and underachieving. Learn to act and be decisive eliminating procrastination from your life.

Be flexible. As you reach for the stars and pursue your dreams, there will be times that the goals you have established for yourself or the way you are approaching them will require change. The fear of change can keep us bound to our comfort zone. Learning this, some set strict goals and leap at them. Thinking they had put it behind them, they return to their changeless ways. This time they refuse from changing their goal.

Goals shouldn't be changed every five minutes, but they shouldn't be written in granite either. An important point in goal setting is evaluating them from time to time. Back to the aiming analogy. Modern military artillery fires shells many miles over the horizon. They don't just aim towards their targets and repeatedly fire. They use forward spotters to radio back the effects of their fire. Did it hit the target, or did it miss. The artillery crew then corrects their aim and fires again.

So we also set our goals and then see how we did. When necessary we take better aim. We might even change our goals completely.

Don't slip back into a fear of change. Don't set goals so rigidly either. Inflexibility will almost guarantee failure.

By now you realize what it takes to be a peak performer and that you have what it takes. You just have to tap into the potential within you. Although there are risks involved when we strive for anything beyond our comfort zone, you need to learn to turn risk into results. Face your fears. Don't be afraid to "go where no man has gone before." Possess imagination, spirit, courage, convictions, responsibility, character, integrity and a perception that stimulates change.

CHANGE YOURSELF
113

STRATEGY 11 : SEVEN : DESTROYERS : OF WEALTH

All of us are constantly striving for financial security, but something always seems to ruin our good intentions. In my dealings with other doctors and business people, a common thread runs through all my conversations with the ones struggling financially. This "thread" consists of seven wealth destroyers that prevent a person from ever accumulating any real money.

Most people are accustomed to hearing about wealth accumulation, saving for the future and financial security in the usual ways. We all know we should save, and we all desire some kind of financial security. If, however, we do not realize the factors at work that subconsciously undermine our efforts, we will never get there. Wealth, although not a quick fix for happiness, will assist us greatly in making things happen in our life. Money is the fuel in the engines that can bring about our success. Who could not use fewer financial worries and more time to spend on things that really matter? Knowing how to save and accumulate wealth can help you achieve this. I'm not talking about marrying a millionaire or answering twenty-one questions on TV. Obsessing on instantly getting more money than you can spend is greed. Developing a plan to accumulate wealth by building up your savings is not.

Study this strategy thoroughly. Understand the wealth destroyers and work on developing a resistance to them. Controlling your finances and creating security is not as difficult as you may think. Whether or not you make a good living is not the real issue. The problem comes not so much in the making of money but rather in the keeping of it. In my business, going from one to twenty-two offices made me realize that basic truth. It seemed the more we collected, the less money we had left over. There was always too much month left at the end of the money.

After many years of counseling others and realizing my own mistakes, I have developed an interest in discovering what causes business failure. Although this strategy is not the only answer, it does touch on what causes so many people to retire broke. Let's take a look at each of the causes in detail as we explore the destroyers of wealth accumulation.

The Seven Wealth Destroyers

1. Relying On Experts with Blind Faith
You will never gain full control of your financial life until you take responsibility for your actions. You need to educate yourself about money and learn all you can about investing, taxes, etc. I emphasize this point over and over again in our seminars. Take taxes for instance. One-third of all your wealth will go to the government in your lifetime. That's more than your home mortgage, your children's education or any other purchase you will make in your lifetime. Yet we spend more time learning about automobiles than the largest expense we will ever have.

I have relied on experts in the past with blind faith and invariably regretted it. You will be amazed at what you can learn if you have a desire to learn it. Don't be fooled into thinking that just because someone holds a degree or a few initials behind their name that they are going to make the right decisions with your money. It just doesn't work that way.

Begin relying on yourself for your financial future. No one will treat your money the way you would handle your own. As a matter of fact, many may handle your money the way they handle *their* own. That, my friend, can be devastating to your financial future and should bring with it much concern. The bottom-line—*rely on yourself.* Seek advice, but make your own decisions based on what you have learned.

2. Financial Complacency
There is nothing wrong with contentment; however, complacency is a deadly destroyer. We stop paying attention and take our eyes off the "eight ball." Before you know it, we are paying the consequences, big consequences. If attaining financial freedom is some-

thing you want, you must remain focused on your goal. Nothing or no one should be allowed to diminish your priority of being the best you can be. Countless people after attaining a measure of financial stability, lose it because of complacency. Thinking *I've made it, I don't have to try anymore* or *I'm just going to set back and let things take care of themselves*, will bring ultimate destruction to one's financial plans. The Bible tells us in the book of Hebrews that being content or happy with today is good. Being complacent is taking contentment to the extreme and, in turn, causes the extreme. Avoid complacency in your financial life. Stay focused and strive to be the best you can be.

3. Lacking Financial Consciousness

This is the number one reason people don't succeed financially. They believe they are not worth the wealth they desire or attain. Believing this way prevents us from attaining financial security and sabotages what we already have.

Many people have grown up hearing certain beliefs about money. Comments like "you can never keep money" and "money is the root of all evil," are well known. Both statements are, however, overstated or misquoted. The Bible says it's the *love* of money, not money itself. But the point is exaggerated because of a fear of greed. The average person does not want to think of himself or herself as greedy. Greed is a vice. I've stated throughout this book that money doesn't guarantee happiness. Unfettered greed will scuttle any chance of success. But acquiring wealth in order to meet your goals is not evil.

Hearing these messages throughout our lives affects our subconscious. We are conditioned against accumulating wealth. People feel an aversion to the subject. The backlash to this conditioning is unfortunate. When a little money comes along, it is quickly spent. There is no plan to get the money. It follows that if there is no plan on how to acquire money, there will be no plan on how to spend it. Quickly it comes; quickly it goes. Automobiles, homes, toys, you name it.

Picture your mind as a thermostat in a room. If the temperature goes up too high the thermostat comes on and cools the room down. If the temperature gets too low, it comes on and warms the room up. This is how our subconscious mind works with money, our business or anything else. If we are within the acceptable boundaries of our mind, everything's okay. But, if we reach the lowest boundary, our gears kick in and we go to work to bring ourselves out of it. If, for instance, our bank balance neared extinction we would be motivated, if not by sheer panic, to action. If, on the other hand, the cash becomes plentiful, more than we need to just get by, it's very easy to begin spending because of our worth value.

Guilt, believing you don't want nor need money, negative associations and the like will all prevent you from reaching and maintaining financial success. Money may not grow on trees, but then again leaves don't grow in your pockets either.

Follow this simple question and answer evaluation to uncover possible hidden attitudes concerning money, and put an end to any self-sabotage that may exist.

Ending Financial Self-Sabotage
1. Recall all of the pain you have experienced because you didn't have the financial abundance you deserve. (Be honest with yourself.)
2. List words that you associate with money. (Be aware of words that conflict with one another such as rich and poor or work and leisure.)
3. Write down what you remember hearing about money when you were growing up, i.e., money can't buy happiness, etc.
4. Write down how your life would be greater and better if money were no longer an issue.
5. Remove your limiting beliefs by associating new and more realistic attitudes towards money. Write these down and say them to yourself over and over again, i.e., money can't buy happiness in and of itself, but it doesn't cause unhappiness either. The lack of money always causes unhappiness.

4. Failure To Have An Effective Strategy
Regardless of who you are you need an effective strategy for reaching your financial goals. Wanting money and watching Carlton

118

Sheets on television alone will not do it. You must step out. You have the means available for accumulating wealth.

We just discussed what happens when you don't have a plan to save money. Often it is spent as soon as it comes in. This book is full of advice on setting goals and carrying out plans for meeting them. Hopefully now you will see just how important it is to have a plan, set goals and carry them out.

It saddens me greatly to see people retire from a life of work that have nothing to show for it. Stay away from all of the off the wall ways to make money. Set a plan to save. Set goals of where you want to be and what you want to do. Then get with the program; follow your plan.

5. Failure to Follow a Plan

I often ask individuals in our seminars if they believe they could save $6.50 a day. Almost always the majority of the room raises their hands. My next question is as simple but doesn't receive the same affirmative answers. "Then, why don't you?" I ask. The average small cap mutual fund yielded somewhere around 16.9% during the years of 1976–1996. If you were to save $6.50 a day or $200 a month at 16% interest, in five years you would have approximately $19,000. In ten years you would have amassed approximately $60,000; 15 years, $150,000; 20 years, $350,000. In 25 years you would be looking at just under one million dollars.

Please understand that I am in no way advocating you take unnecessary risks or that you would receive this type of return if you did. What I am saying is to formulate a plan and stick to it no matter what. Your plan may encompass a more conservative approach. Regardless of whether you are conservative and invest in high-grade municipal bonds or a more aggressive vehicle, the principle is the same.

Most people that start a savings plan soon abandoned it. Unless you win the lottery (which can be devastating if you suffer from a lack of financial consciousness as described above) or inherit a family fortune you must have a plan and *follow it through*. Don't let procrastination be the death of your financial future. If you haven't begun, the time is now.

119

6. Never Making Having Money an Absolute Must

Some individuals stay at a certain weight their entire lives although they would like to be somewhere else. Likewise, you may stay at the same financial level unless you make having money a must. That doesn't mean it comes before everything in your life. It just means it must be important to you.

Again, money is just a tool. It is a tool with a stigma attached, however. Making having money a must may repulse you. But it is important. Money is a requirement for living. Corporations, ministries and households all need it. A hammer can be used for good or evil. It can build your house; it can hurt someone. Money is as essential in building your dreams as it is to the carpenter building a house. It needs to have the right priority in your life.

In order to make that a reality, discipline must be at the core of your vocabulary. If your mentality is money doesn't really mean that much to me, then it won't. It will never be a problem for you. You just won't have any to worry about.

I hear this all the time. "All I want to do is just pay my bills." "I don't need much money, just enough to get by." There's an old saying that says, "If you ask for something enough, you may get it."

I firmly believe that we shouldn't allow words out of our mouth that we don't mean. Be very careful what you say and equally cautious of what you think. Remember attitude determines altitude. Guard your mouth and your heart. If you desire to have money in your life, your words and actions must produce it. Abundance leads to abundance. Make your goal having your money work for you rather than you working for it by having the right attitude about money.

7. Allowing Financial Crisis to Turn into Financial Ruin

This is the final kicker. Understanding this stage and truly accepting it is imperative even if you live by the other six stages.

We all are faced with situations involving financial crisis in our lives. How we handle them separates the financially successful from the financial failures. If failure comes, accept it. Make some necessary changes. Then get up and try again. You are only truly out of the game when you quit. Continue to pursue your passion.

When I was left with a bank account $50,000 in the red, accounts payable over $200,000 and a seven-figure debt after a nasty partnership break-up, I felt like jumping off of a bridge. By facing it and using it to my advantage it has become a learning experience that has enabled me to help others. Without that crisis I would have never been exposed to the things that I have. Neither would I have had the privilege of helping so many people.

This stage creates the financial death rattle, which is an excuse not to try anymore. None of us enjoy pain. As a matter of fact, avoiding pain is human nature. People are afraid of the unknown, but when faced with it, we find that it is a much smaller beast than we thought.

In summary, the question must lie with you. Do you want to help others, help yourself, your family and give to needy causes? If the answer is yes you, need the money to make it become a reality.

Sir John Templeton, founder of Templeton mutual funds, was once asked what his key to wealth was. His answer was simple yet profound. "Gratitude," he said. You can have all the money in the world and be miserable but not if you're grateful and realize who you are, where you came from and where you're ultimately going.

Ninety-five percent of people in the U.S. at the age of 65 are broke. Eighty-five out of one hundred Americans at the age of 65 cannot put their hands on $250 in cash![†]

Make it a point not to be a statistic. Understand these seven basic wealth destroyers, and make attaining financial freedom one of your main goals in life. Only by making it important will you see it become a reality.

[†]Statistics from "MOORE For Your Money." A financial newsletter by Byron R. Moore, CFP.

CHANGE YOURSElF
123

STRATEGY 12 : ELIMINATING FEAR

Fear is not a subject that many want to talk about. As a matter of fact, most deny fear's effect in their lives. What is it that makes fear such a taboo subject? The primary reason is pride. People as a whole are too prideful to admit they are afraid of something or that a specific fear is preventing them from accomplishing a certain task.

Peak performers eliminate fear from their lives. I realize that is easier said than done, but this step is crucial. Fear will block you from capitalizing on any opportunities that comes your way.

Fear in the negative sense is the appearance of something much larger and capable of harm than it actually is. Fear comes in two different forms. The first is the fear of failure. We have spoken about the willingness to fail and its importance to your success. Fear of failure keeps many from reaching their dreams. Overcoming and accepting some risk when necessary is key to becoming the person you want to be. Getting up when we fall down makes us who we are and forms our character in life.

What if the fear of failing keeps us from doing something that we should do? Failure is not a destination but an event. It is no one's destiny to fail. You never arrive there. Failure happens, sometimes by our hands. At other times failure happens because of circumstances beyond our control. However, we don't get stuck there.

Time is a wonderful ally when we see failure as an event, not as a destination. Failure happens at a certain point in time. One moment we realize it. The next moment we feel its effects. But the clock doesn't stop there. The second hand keeps on ticking, even though we feel stuck in time. Actually that moment of failure keeps slipping further into the past.

Think of it this way. We all live our lives on boats in the river of time. The boat never stops; it takes us ever forward. When failure strikes we drop something over the side of the boat. We look at it now in the water with shock. We ask how it happened. We scold ourselves. We grieve; we become angry. All along the object starts floating further away from us. Each second takes it a greater distance behind our boat. After awhile we don't even see it anymore.

Time carries us on past the event of our failure. We're not stuck there. We're free to try again. Realize that it was something at a point of time and move on.

Looking at failure this way keeps us from fearing it. No one wants to fail. But realizing that if we do—or even when we do—we won't find ourselves at the end of the road. We have the opportunity to learn from it and watch it slip out of sight far behind us.

The second form of fear is the fear of rejection. If we are fortunate enough to overcome the fear of failure, rejection still lurks around the corner. Many people are living a life as we described in strategy nine due to their fear of rejection.

There is an analogy that I use quite frequently concerning rejection that sheds a different light on it. Pretend for a moment that you are asleep and are awakened by a knocking on your door. You get up and open the door finding a man standing there with a vacuum cleaner in his hand. He begins to tell you that the vacuum cleaner is capable of cleaning everything from fingernails to cat hair and he would like to demonstrate it for you. What would be your response? Pretend further that it's 1:00 in the morning. Would you be polite and let him in? I realize that everyone's response is different, but I would venture to say that you would say no and ask him to leave—politely!

Let's use the same scenario, same time of the day, etc. The only difference is that he has had car trouble and his family is stranded. He asks you to call a phone number he gives to you and apologizes for any inconvenience he may have caused you. He appreciates any help you could give him by simply calling for help. Remember, same man, same time of day but different circumstances.

What would you do now? Would you respond differently? Most of us would. What was different? In one scenario we were rejecting someone and in the other we were accepting the same person. The difference is what you need to understand about rejection. You weren't rejecting the man; you were rejecting what he was selling.

I have told that story on numerous occasions and have yet to get a different response. We accept what we understand and perceive not to be a threat to us. If we could only take this analogy to heart, I am convinced that it could change the way we look at life and the fear of rejection.

Fear stands for nothing more than *False Evidence Appearing Real.* You can look the world over and you will find there is only one way to overcome fear of any kind: You must face it head on. By turning our heads we sabotage our success and therefore sabotage our lives. One of the saddest sights you will ever see is a person that has accepted failure as the ultimate destination for their life. God didn't create any losers. You were created to win. Allowing a crisis to transform your life into something that you are not is an existence that will kill you without taking your life.

Only confrontation eliminates fear. Working with doctors in our profession, generally the more confrontational ones enjoy more success. They have no problem telling someone what they need to hear instead of what they think they will accept.

We do the same thing in life. We tend to do and say things that we think are pleasing to others when that may not necessarily be what they need to hear. Would you want your doctor to only prescribe treatments he thought you could afford? I want to know the truth no matter how painful it might be.

As peak performers we must be willing to accept no as an answer without the feeling of rejection. You will never know unless you ask, and you will never receive either. To confront fear, especially the fear of rejection, asking is a well-known cure. The more you ask the more comfortable you become with asking and, in turn, the better you are at accepting no as an answer. Mark Victor Hansen has a book titled *The Aladdin Factor* that does an excellent job at explaining the phenomenon of asking and receiving. The Bible itself speaks of it, stating that if we ask we will receive. To better understand fear and its silent effects, below I have listed what fear is and is not.

Fear is:
- Silent in nature.
- A thief of life's dreams.

- One of the major causes of excuse-it-itis.
- A destroyer of self-esteem.
- A mountain that *appears* to be insurmountable.

Fear is not:

- An alarm system that informs you that you are afraid.
- A success-achieving trait.
- A reason for not trying.
- A builder of self-image.
- A little bump in the road to achieving your goals.

You may possess several factors that insure failure. Look out for doubt, procrastination, excuses, greed, and laziness. Yielding to any one of them can keep you from reaching the goals you have established for your life.

When speaking to people about fear I find they are not fearful after all. They usually are just uncomfortable doing certain things. As a result they avoid doing them. A lack of will to confront often causes this avoidance.

It puzzled me when I could replace a struggling doctor with a successful one and see no results. The environment that struggled continued to do so. This motivated me to study this phenomenon in detail. Then I came upon the concept of positive confrontation, or the persuading to look at your beliefs. The macho Rambo attitude won't work here. This is not a take no prisoners approach. It is just the opposite.

The fear of rejection is actually the fear of confrontation or *carefronting*; a term coined by my good friend Mrs. Vi Bryant. This lack of desire to ask what we wish to have, tell it like it is and explain the facts is the number one reason for fear among most people. I have watched doctors tell a patient that they needed a specific amount of care and explain the cost as if it were a well-known fact. On the other hand, other doctors beat around the bush, saying everything else but what a patient needed to hear. Likewise, I have seen people raise positive kids in this negative world simply by carefronting the issues and not avoiding them. For instance, not talking about drugs and sex is not going to make it go away. As a matter of fact it may very well make it worse.

Have you ever felt uncomfortable with something that you know would probably bring you more business or enhance your life in some way? I'm not talking about something illegal or even immoral. Something gives you a twinge to think about. You hesitate or even try to avoid the issue. Then you have experienced the confrontation issue.

So how do you advance yourself beyond that point? There are several ways to build up your ability to confront. The first is to *act as if* you are what you want to become by doing what it is you are most uncomfortable doing. I am not saying to sing someone else's song. You must be yourself. The problem is that we really don't realize what we are designed to be and do until we step out and try.

When I am asked what can be done to build a business, the first thing I do is to go through the gamut of items that would build the business as well as the individual. The thing the person is most uncomfortable with is generally the thing I will ask them to do. There are several results to this exercise. One is that it causes the individual to *carefront* the things he or she is most afraid of. It allows him to realize that no one is going to bite you and that there is nothing wrong with "no."

Another benefit to this exercise is the obvious end result of increased productivity. It never ceases to amaze me when a person asks for help but is unwilling to accept advice when it is given. It's almost as if a secret is being looked for and until it is found I will remain the way I am. Remember, continuing to do the same things over and over, expecting different results, is insanity. Don't fall prey to it.

The second thing you can do is to *be accountable to someone.* Accountability is imperative in the remedy of fear elimination and confrontational growth. You have to find someone of like mind that is understanding of you (i.e. a mentor or close friend). Having someone hold you accountable will bring you that much closer to your goal. You would be absolutely amazed at what this simple procedure can do for your life.

Last, *continue to work at your ability to communicate and confront.* Confrontation is not a skill that you learn and never have to work at anymore. It takes continual practice to be able to confront without just conflicting.

With a better understanding of what causes fear in our lives, I have listed below a list of questions to assist you in *carefronting* your confrontation. Please review them closely and answer them honestly. To do anything less will only cheat yourself and prevent you from breaking out of the prison of fear and dreams with no action.

Confronting Fear Exercise

1. List some times in your life where you remember having problems confronting an issue (i.e., talking to my kids about drugs, asking for assistance in some area of my life, closing a sale, accepting food prepared at a restaurant in a different way than you requested, etc.).

_____

_____

_____

_____

_____

2. List the things you believe are holding you back from confronting issues that are important in your life.

_____

_____

_____

_____

_____

3. Write out an action plan to assist you in rectifying this problem.

_____

_____

_____

_____

4. To whom will you be accountable?

_____

_____

_____

_____

As you complete this exercise you will find there may be more things in your life hindering you from attaining success than you thought. Most who understand this concept soon realize that it is the action step necessary to breaking through the barriers keeping us from peak performance.

Think of how you make a living. There are basically three ways. The first is by using your muscle. You can shovel, lift, drive trucks, pick, build, etc for a specific wage. The pay is usually low because the risk is low. The next way of earning money is by using your brain. Brainwork is used with professions such as accounting and engineering. These types of professions do pay a decent wage. The last way to earn money is by "emotional risk" or having a tolerance for rejection. These types of people do not take the path of least resistance. They realize that the higher the reward the higher the risk. In the emotional risk category you will find everything from salesman to doctors and lawyers. This category carries with it the highest level of compensation. Individuals under this banner are not concerned with hearing "no" because they understand they will eventually hear a "yes."

Most of the success stories I have discussed in this book fall into the emotional risk category. They are not afraid of getting their feelings hurt. Remember the old saying, "no pain, no gain?" There was truth to it after all. Some of the highest incomes reported to the IRS each year are from those that take the risk necessary to receive the prize. When I first heard of this emotional risk/confrontation idea, I thought it was a bunch of words placed together just to sound good. Not so. It is as real as success and failure is. The willingness to fail is, without doubt, the willingness to succeed.

So what about this fear thing? If I realize what *carefronting* is and continue to face it head on, will I still experience fear? The answer is yes. The reality is the fear will seem much smaller than it appeared before you first confronted it. Some feel that regardless of which way they turn, nothing they do can eliminate their fear.

I once heard a story of a doctor that requested help with his practice. He was told several things he should do. One was to raise his fees, but he couldn't do that because his staff was against it. He was also told that he should cut the salaries of his employees, but that wouldn't work because they would all quit and boycott his office. Finally, he was told that he should consider letting one of his staff members go. That was quickly rejected with the thought that no one would come in to see him because everyone liked his staff so much they would reject him for his un-founded decision. Of course his wife would kill him if he did not make more money and make it fast. Regardless of which way he turned he was doomed.

This is known as the confrontational box. Answers, but no hope. Advice, but none that pertains to the situation at hand. For those individuals that find themselves in this box there is little hope until it is recognized. The only way out is to find the door. Leave without looking back.

In my book *True Prosperity* I've listed five areas that must be avoided to overcome failure. For the sake of understanding them and for those that haven't read it, I have listed them for your reference below.

Uncontrollable frustration. Regardless of who you are and how well established, you may be there will always be frustration in your life. The key is learning to control it. The closer you get to your goal the more important it is to learn how to control your frustration. I don't know of anyone that has ever achieved a status in life that frustration no longer becomes a factor. Every success story has mounds and mounds of frustration as part of its formula. As individuals striving for peak performance this area becomes even more important. Learning to control frustration yields big dividends. All successful people must dig through the frustration to find success.

It doesn't matter whether it is your family or a business decision, with each frustration there is a learning experience. Controlling frustration is, for all practical purposes, a major key to success achievement and peak performance.

Avoiding rejection. Allowing a fear of rejection to dictate your course sets the stage for failure. Taking the path of least resistance will only give you the least life has to offer. Show me a peak performer, and I will show you someone who has taken the path of confrontation and emotional risk. Remember, all someone can do is say no, and with no you are in good company.

Avoiding financial pressure. No matter how long you have been in business or how much money you have, you will ultimately face financial pressure in your lifetime. Avoiding financial pressure will only lead to destruction. Again we are faced with the ultimate answer, confrontation. Face your pressures head on. Making decisions based on financial pressure alone doesn't guarantee success. Weigh all your risks, but don't fear it. Financial pressure is worth living with if there are promised benefits.

Complacency. I have seen it so many times. Someone has worked their whole life, and finally they have reached the pinnacle. No more worry, no more work. Just sit back and let it happen on it's own. Granted we shouldn't worry, but to become complacent and no longer try is the ultimate formula for failure. Once you get the ball rolling you have to continue to give it a shove in the right direction or else it will either stop rolling or roll the wrong way. Be content with who you are and where you are, but do not allow yourself to think laziness will keep you moving in the right direction. That's your responsibility.

Greed. The very word should tell you the danger of allowing it to take hold of your life. I have personally witnessed people who allow greed to take over and end up where they first started in life. Greed is like a cancer. It will eat you up little by little sometimes with no notice whatsoever. Peak performers realize that the remedy for greed is giving. Learn to make giving a part of your life. Remove the "what's in it for me" mentality, and began looking for what you can do for others. I can assure you that not only will your life be better because of it, you will also be contributing to a better world. What a better way to make things happen in your life than to make a difference in the world? Become a giver and soon you will be a receiver.

Fear produces the outcome of most situations in our life. For example, if we expect to get ill, we usually do. I have known people that have feared a certain age because that was the age that their dad died or someone close to them. The legendary rock and roll singer, Elvis Presley died at the same age as his mother from the same thing. "I hate this time of year because I always get a cold," usually produces just that.

This kind of result from our foreboding is called *the law of expectation*. It can be used negatively as is demonstrated in this example. It can also be used positively. If we expect the best we more often get what we desire than if we expect the worse. We eliminate fear by facing it over and over again until the fear reveals it's true identity, which is a sheep in wolf's clothing. Confront your fear and your fear will cease to confront you.

In summary, realize that most fears are created by our unwillingness to step out of our comfort zone. Fight your giants as David did in the Bible. Regardless of their size they will all fall if confronted with confidence and wisdom. The elimination of negative fear in your life, the kind that prevents you from becoming and doing all you are capable of, will bring you into the ring with the peak performers of this world and ultimately into the winner's circle of life.

CHANGE YOURSELF

135

STRATEGY 13 : LEARN : TO : COMMUNICATE

Communication is the key to all relationships. It is the very essence of understanding each other. Without communication accomplishing anything would be impossible. Yet many of us function just in that manner, without communicating. We talk, we look and we hear, but seldom do we listen to anything that is being said.

If we look at our basic anatomy, we realize that God gave us two ears and two eyes so that we could listen and see twice as much as we talk. Most of us use our mouths twice as much as we should. We blab continuously without a care of what the other person is trying to communicate to us. I get amused when watching people sitting in a restaurant. We've all seen the couple looking at each other from across the table. Their silent stares only momentarily interrupted by a couple of occasional words.

You can tell when someone is really listening to you. If you look closely at their gestures and into their eyes, you immediately know whether they are with you or not. Peak performers survive on their effective communication skills. As these develop we become better leaders and have more successful relationships.

We all need companionship. Although practically anyone can find a companion, few reach the pinnacle of success in experiencing true relationships, the kind that last for a lifetime. When I think of what my wife and children add to my life, I am reminded again that the things that matter the most in life are the things that money can't buy.

As we strive to reach the top by performing at our peak, we can't take our eyes off of the things that matter most. Learning this will catapult you to a level that most only dream of. Many mistake the key to success as a mystery. Often they ask an important person, What is the *secret* of your success. Hopefully what you have read so far in this book has enabled you to see that there are no secrets, just facts, principles and hard work. Communication is one of those areas that require hard work to develop. We talked much about leadership in strategy six.

Effective communication really is the key to all relationships. Whether you are a corporate executive or a greeter at a major department store how you come across to others will make or break a company. It will also make or break a relationship. Most marriages have difficulty due to a lack of communication.

Zig Ziglar tells a story about communication that sheds a humorous light on a serious subject. A woman went to her attorney for a divorce. Upon questioning the lady the attorney asked if she woke up grumpy in the morning. The lady responded, "no I don't wake him up he gets up himself!" The attorney was confused by her answer but proceeded to ask the next question. "Does he beat you up?" asked the attorney. "No," she replied in a huffy tone "I get up before him at least two hours everyday." By this time the attorney was beginning to loose his patience when he asked, "Do you have a grudge?" The lady replied, "We have a small one that only fits two cars!" Finally the attorney asked, "Why are you getting a divorce?" The lady said it all with her final reply; "We just can't communicate!"

Isn't that the case in many instances? We feel lost when we can't seem to find the right words to express our feelings. We get frustrated, feel misunderstood and often give up. It takes two to communicate. Both parties share the responsibility when communication fails. Since you are not responsible for the other person, be responsible for yourself. Take charge of your communication by improving your communication skills. The first step may be considering yourself as the problem when difficulty arises. Speak not to get things off your chest, but speak to communicate. Do so in a way that the other person understands. Consider it your job to articulate your message in a way that will be easily comprehended. Don't consider it the other person's job to Wgure it out.

I so often hear the question, How do you get everything done each day? I'll bet you have asked yourself that same question before as well. We have discussed the importance of delegation in a previous strategy, but what good does delegating do if we can't communicate what we really want. Communicating effectively requires following these few easy steps.

Steps to Communicate Effectively

Make eye to eye contact. Looking at the person speaking to you in the eyes is one of the greatest compliments you can give the speaker. It also shows that you are an effective listener, which is a sign of a peak performer. Looking away, occasionally nodding or grunting does not constitute listening. Don't overlook eye to eye contact in your communication. It shows your willingness to listen and your consideration for what is being said. Last but not least it builds up your tolerance to *carefront,* discussed in strategy twelve.

Pay attention to the physical gestures of others. You can tell a lot about how well people are listening to you by the way they carry themselves during a conversation. Arms crossing, constant movement, etc. are signs of a person that is either tired of what you have to say or they are in disagreement with you. Whichever the case, be aware of the other person's attitude, how he or she is receiving you. Communicate in a language that they can understand and interact with.

Many times simply applying a few techniques makes all the difference. Speak with the same tone as the other person (unless they are angry). Be relaxed as you converse. Acknowledge what is said to you. Let the other person know she is communicating, that she is being heard.

Don't stare. Eye contact is important, as we have stated earlier. Staring, however, is an entirely different matter. That's eye contact taken too far. Things can become unnatural if you're not use to looking someone square in the eye. One can overcompensate. Staring can be intimidating. It can be misunderstood for being confrontational. It's a communication killer. If you notice the other person seeming uncomfortable, try a bit less eye contact. You'll soon come to a balance.

Acknowledge what is being said. Nothing is more annoying than thinking someone is not paying attention to you. You've been talking for a while when it occurs to you: Hey that dude is daydreaming! Communication is something like what the Army calls *firing for effect*. You let go a few artillery shells to see what you hit. You then make tiny adjustment to your aim until you're on target. When you communicate, you let go a salvo of phrases. You look at the other person to see if you are hitting the target. The target is the other person understanding what you're trying to say. When you don't acknowledge what someone else says, the other person doesn't have an idea how close to the target he or she is getting. Smile when appropriate, nod your head when you understand and acknowledge what is being said to you. Wait at least three to five seconds before speaking. Make sure the other person is done first. And never highjack the conversation. When someone is talking about something and you launch in another direction, who can tell if you were even listening. You certainly didn't acknowledge as much.

Learn to be agreeable by accepting others opinions. Yes you heard it right. Learn to agree with people more than you disagree. People generally avoid those that are constantly looking for an argument. That doesn't mean that you should give up your values or your beliefs. Still it is a good idea to make a conscious effort to not offer your opinion every chance you get. Listen more and talk less. If people are avoiding you on a regular basis, maybe you should consider this. They may think you have a strong opinionated spirit. Don't offer you opinion just because you have one. Don't confront people just because their position is different from yours. Usually if someone feels as strongly as you do, you are not going to change his or her mind anyway.

Accepting other's opinions doesn't mean you are actually agreeing with them. What you reflect by the way you live will have a much greater effect than what you say. People need to see values in your actions not your words.

The above steps will help you communicate, but the surest way to better communication is become a better listener. Learn to listen.

Listening is an art. It is the way you show value in what another person has to say.

There are three main benefits to listening. The first is *trust*. Whenever someone listens to us we develop a sense of trust. The more actively one listens to the other the faster the bond of trust builds. Good listeners are more persuasive. They garner more respect. Their opinions have more impact when they are asked for.

The second benefit is that *listening builds self-esteem*. When you carefully listen to the other person, his or her self-esteem goes up. Likewise whenever someone listens carefully to you, your self-esteem goes up. You feel more important.

The third benefit of listening is *self-discipline*. It requires a significant amount of self-control to listen actively to another person. The average person speaks about 150 words a minute while you can listen at a rate of almost 600 words per minute. To actively listen you must control your attention and remain focused. The more you discipline yourself by listening the more controlled you will be in other areas of your life.

The last part of communication that we will discuss in creating peak performance is how to resolve conflict. How many people really enjoy conflict? Rarely is conflict useful. It can keep you bound in frustration and unproductively.

Conflict can be defined as:
1. A competitive or opposing action of incompatibles.
2. Mental struggles resulting from incompatible or opposing needs, drives, wishes, or eternal or internal demands.
3. A hostile encounter.
4. To show antagonism or irreconcilable differences.

The main problems causing conflict usually revolve around the three centers of life namely *time, money* or *sex.* Of all the areas concerning communication for the peak performer none is more pertinent than conflict. Our tongues get us into more trouble than any other part of our body. Although it is the smallest part, it is the one that can produce the most damage. If you want to know just how important controlling your tongue is read the book of James in the Bible. So many people have destroyed their lives because of words they wish they never said.

I know. I was one of them. Although I did not allow it to destroy my life, I came very close. What haunts me to this day is not what I almost did to me. It chills my spine to think of what my words did to others. I never realized the trauma I caused by my careless speech. I would never knowingly hurt anyone. But I had allowed stress to so influence my speech that each biting word cut into others.

Anyone trying to be successful in such a situation is entering the boxing ring with both hands tied behind his back. Such conduct was damaging to me and everything I valued. I have learned my lesson. Don't let harsh words sabotage you. Don't let stress and conflict torpedo your ability to communicate.

The purpose of this strategy is not to condemn you, but to help you realize where you are and what you need to do to change your direction. You can deal powerfully with conflict through communication. Take a look at the following steps.

Seven Steps to Resolving Conflict

1. **Agree on a time and a place to talk.** Take control of the situation. Don't let flare-ups and tempers feed chaos. Having a plan will cool things down. Calmer heads will prevail rather than if you tried to work things out on the spur of the moment. The time and place should be no longer than 48 hours and preferably before the sun goes down.

2. **Spell out the ground rules and stick by them.** Stick to the subject. Many times we argue and aren't even arguing about the real issue. Don't allow yourself to wander off the main subject. As for rules, follow these simple instructions. *Time rule:* 15–30 minutes. Any longer only allows a redundancy in the conversation. *Time out:* Take time out if you began to cross over and become personal. One way to resolve conflict is to avoid it. *Listen actively: Be* sure you listen to every word being said. Validate the other person by acknowledging his issues. Steven Covey once said a statement that pertains well to the above. "Seek first to

understand and then to be understood." What great words when it comes to conflict resolution.

3. **Identify the problem.** Be sure you know what it is you are talking about. Many times people enter into a conversation to resolve a matter and not even know what they are resolving. Get on the same page. Start by each one involved articulating the problem. It is crucial to start on common ground.

4. **Validate each other and then the relationship.** Look for the positive in each other and in the relationship. Regardless of whether it is a spouse or a co-worker, looking for the positive will assist in resolving a matter much faster than dwelling on the negative.

5. **Discuss possible solutions.** First you can capitulate and give in. If that is not an option, perhaps you can compromise. The last option is to learn to co-exist or agree to disagree. If you choose this option I would encourage you to revisit the issue from time to time.

6. **Pray.** Prayer is known to heal more conflict than any other item. It soothes the soul and allows a humbling of the spirit. Make it a part of conflict resolution and your life.

7. **Carry out the solution.** Move forward, and do the things you say you are going to do. Steps to resolving conflict do no good unless you are willing to carry them out to the end. Not doing so is what makes talk cheap. Take the common ground gained and reinforce it. Do not lose it if you can help it. From that ground, start working toward your resolution.

As you can see, communication is a complicated subject, but it doesn't have to be a complicated part of your life. Understanding the art of communication can assist you greatly in business, negotiations, relationships and leadership roles. It literally can make or break the achievement of a peak performer.

Make learning to communicate a part of your life. Make it an absolute must. The path that good communication leads to in life is that of those that make things happen in their life. Think of the first time you drove a car. You had to think of every move you were going to make. With some additional practice and guidance, you were able to drive competently. However, you had to be consciously aware of what you were doing with all the mechanical aspects of the car as well as your body. You had to be aware of monitoring the traffic behind you, turning your blinkers on and staying on the right side of the road just to mention a few of the things associated with driving.

Now, think of the last time that you drove a car. Everything fell into place. You didn't think about any of those details that you did the first time. This is the level where we can do something well and not even have to think about it. It comes naturally.

CHANGE YOURSELF

145

STRATEGY : FORGET
14 : LEANING AND
: BEGIN LIFTING

Now that you have almost completed the strategies for becoming a peak performer, it is important that we understand the difference between lifting and leaning. This will be the shortest of the strategies in this book. I set out to write a complex discussion on lifting others up. It occurred to me that encouragement shouldn't be that artificial. In fact it is quite natural. It's not just something we learn, but in reality something we let loose from within. It's the part of us we want to show but are afraid to. However, as a peak performer we can't let fear get in our way of doing what is right.

Most relationships are a mixture of two modes: giving and taking. When you relate to people you give life. Sometimes, however, you take life. It is necessary to do both in the healthy relationships in your life. We all have times of need. In those times we lean. It is expected.

The problem surfaces when a relationship becomes all one mode, all giving or all taking. We all know people that are so needy that they are always takers. They suck the life right out of you. Seldom do they give.

Another mode of relating lies somewhere in between. They don't take, but neither do they give. This mode exists for mutual benefit. It resembles a business transaction. These people deal with each other to get something. But since they expect the other person to benefit, it is not considered taking. It's a mutual transaction.

Many people operate on this level, never giving. Their best friends are the people they work with, not because they are deep relationships but because they are the only relationships. If they weren't forced to be with these people, then they would not be relating in the first place. These type of relationship where there is no giving is unfulfilling.

There are many benefits to life-giving relationships. George Bailey, the main character in the perennial favorite "It's a Wonderful Life," spent his life lifting others. Sacrificing himself, he made a way for others. When at his lowest point, he found out that he was the riches man in town. Not that his bank statement said so, he was valued because he made a difference in people's lives.

There was a song years ago with the lyric "you were the wind beneath my wings." Things with wings fly because air moves beneath them. This causes lift. Many people go through life flapping their wings like a chicken. They become tired before they get across the barnyard. Eagles, on the other hand, seek out currents. They stretch out their wings and soar. When we encourage others we enable them to soar; we give them lift.

Peak performers lift. They assist each other in reaching for the sky, moving forward and never looking back.

The majority of this world is made up of people who lean. Leaning on others is okay to a certain extent; however, we tend to carry it to the extreme. So what is the answer? I believe that we must begin to look at the world as a place to give not just to take. The taking mentality causes people to dump on each other, never thinking of lifting each other up.

By now you realize that in order to make things happen you have to be cautious of what you allow in your head and eventually into your heart. To *change yourself* as the table of content states implies the missing ingredient between those who wish and those who get. Of equal importance is allowing others to see you as someone they want to be around, someone they feel will lift them up. Being known as a lifter is the icing on the cake for the peak performer.

I realize the title of this strategy is to forget leaning, but the implication is to lean only when necessary and only for the purpose of lifting ourselves up. When we finally find the recovery we are looking for we should be prepared to stop holding the warm blanket and begin lifting others up in their time of need.

The deepest need of humans is to be needed. We think we are burdening a friend when in all actuality we are not. Most of us want to help others. We just need to be told when *we* are needed to be

148

lifters. It takes humility to express pain and honesty to express it truly. If you need to lean on someone and can't, think about why. Usually there is some anger, guilt, fear, or pride. I'm talking about in its destructive form. The Bible talks explicitly about pride leading to destruction. Here again it is a destructive pride or *egotism.*

In our church we have small group meetings in people's homes. The purpose is to help out each other. We lift one another as well as lean. Here are some strategies that can assist you in becoming a lifter.

Strategies for Being a Lifter

Avoid gossip. It is so easy to talk about others but what does it accomplish? If you are going to be a lifter it is imperative that you disassociate yourself from people who get their kicks out of taking stabs at others. Negative talk will only produce negativity and, in turn, cause you to see opportunities as stumbling blocks.

Look for the positive in the negative. There will always be things that don't turn out the way you wanted. Learn to appreciate the positive in every situation, even the worst. You are not denying the negative, but accentuating the positive. The human race is known to like dirty laundry. Looking at the positive in someone can give him or her the break to turn his or her situation around.

Develop a caring attitude. Most individuals care about the feelings of others, but very few know how to express it. I have seen people project a non-caring attitude when they actually believe they are being sympathetic. We tend to grow cold over the years. We become accustomed to things going about our business like nothing is wrong.

The fact of the matter is that there is something wrong. Someone is hurting. Someone needs your help.

We need not only to love but also to be loved. Develop a caring attitude. Look people in the eyes, and show you care. Above all, really listen to what is being said.

Sometime ago I was introduced to a poem that I thought summarized this subject very well. It is, for all practical purposes, the core of this strategy. Below you will find the a portion of this poem by Ella Wheeler Wikcox entitled "Two Kinds of People." It is one of my favorite poems. I hope it along with the strategies of this book brings you closer to becoming the peak performer that God Himself designed you to be.

Making positive things happen in your life is now up to you. You have the tools and the strategies to follow. All it takes now is the will. I pray you find that desire and that one-day in the not so distant future you can honestly say you are creating the life you have always dreamed of.

Remember that God loves you no matter who you are. If people tell you different, pay no attention to them. *You* are special because there is only one of you. If you are living your life contrary to what God designed for you, then change! You can make a difference when you finally make up your mind to do so.

May God in all of His infinite wisdom bless and guide you as you strive to *MAKE IT HAPPEN* in your life.

Two Kinds of People

There are two kinds of people of earth today,
Just two kinds of people, no more I say.
Not the good and the bad, for 'tis well
understood,
That the good are half-bad and the bad are
half-good.
No! The two kinds of people on earth I mean,
Are the people who lift and the people who
lean.

— Ella Wheeler Wikcox

⦂ ABOUT
⦂ THE
⦂ AUTHOR

Dr. Dallas Humble is a 1982 graduate of Palmer College in Davenport, Iowa. He served as President of the Chiropractic Association of Louisiana in 1993–94. In 1998, he was honored with the Barnabus Award in recognition for his impact in Christian ministry. Dr. Humble is the president of Dallas Humble, Inc. (DHI), a company aimed at building businesses by building lives. Presently he owns and operates a multiple chiropractic clinic practice. He is a leading authority on creating change and success in people's lives.

Dr. Humble is a prolific writer addressing professional development, leadership and motivational issues. He has authored several books including *True Prosperity: Achieving Success in a World of Failure* and *Make It Happen: Strategies for Achieving Peak Performance in Your Life.*

He is a highly sought after seminar teacher and speaker and is active in his church and community. Dr. Humble resides in North Louisiana with his wife, Diane, and their three children, Zachary, Skyler and Payton.

ORDER FORM

Phone Orders
Call toll free:
800-282-1974 ext. 150

Postal Orders
Dallas Humble
3602 Cypress Street
West Monroe, LA 71291

Fax Orders
318-397-9627

Name _____

Address _____

City _____ ST _____ Zip _____

Phone _____ Email _____

Payment   ☐Check   ☐Credit Card

Credit Card No. _____

Exp. Date _____

Signature _____

Please Send The Following Books:
☐ *Make it Happen* ($10.95)   Qty: _____
☐ *True Prosperity* ($12.95)   Qty: _____

Shipping:

$2.00 for the first book.
$1.00 each additional book.

ORDER FORM

Phone Orders
Call toll free:
800-282-1974 ext. 150

Postal Orders
Dallas Humble
3602 Cypress Street
West Monroe, LA 71291

Fax Orders
318-397-9627

Name _____

Address _____

City _____ ST _____ Zip _____

Phone _____ Email _____

Payment   ☐ Check   ☐ Credit Card

Credit Card No. _____

Exp. Date _____

Signature _____

Please Send The Following Books:
☐ *Make it Happen* ($10.95)   Qty: _____
☐ *True Prosperity* ($12.95)   Qty: _____

Shipping:
$2.00 for the first book.
$1.00 each additional book.

ORDER FORM

Phone Orders
Call toll free:
800-282-1974 ext. 150

Fax Orders
318-397-9627

Postal Orders
Dallas Humble
3602 Cypress Street
West Monroe, LA 71291

Name _____

Address _____

City _____ ST _____ Zip _____

Phone _____ Email _____

Payment   ☐Check   ☐Credit Card

Credit Card No. _____

Exp. Date _____

Signature _____

Please Send The Following Books:
☐ *Make it Happen* ($10.95)   Qty: _____
☐ *True Prosperity* ($12.95)   Qty: _____

Shipping:
$2.00 for the first book.
$1.00 each additional book.